William McDonals

Songs of joy and gladness

William McDonals

Songs of joy and gladness

ISBN/EAN: 9783337265199

Printed in Europe, USA, Canada, Australia, Japan

Cover: Foto ©Thomas Meinert / pixelio.de

More available books at **www.hansebooks.com**

BY

W. McDONALD,

JOSHUA GILL,

JNO. R. SWENEY,

W. J. KIRKPATRICK.

———————

PUBLISHED BY McDONALD & GILL,

36 BROMFIELD STREET, BOSTON.

PREFACE.

———◄►———

"Songs of Joy and Gladness" will speak, or perhaps we should say, sing for itself. It has been prepared with great care, at great expense, and has been revised by competent hands. This treasury contains "things new and old." Happy will he be who can "bring them forth."

McDONALD & GILL.

T. H. Lenfest, Music Typographer, School St., Boston.

SONGS OF JOY AND GLADNESS.

1   All for Jesus!

Words by MARY D. JAMES.   (For Male Voices.)   Music by ASA HULL.

1st & 2d TENOR.

1. All for Je - sus! all for Je - sus! All my being's ransom'd pow'rs;

1st & 2d BASS.

All my thoughts and words and doings, All my days and all my hours.

Repeat pp Rit. second time.

All for Je - sus! All for Je - sus! All my days and all my hours.

2 Let my hands perform his bidding;
  Let my feet run in his ways;
Let my eyes see Jesus only;
  Let my lips speak forth his praise.
    All for Jesus! all for Jesus!
    Let my lips speak forth his praise.

3 Worldlings prize their gems of beauty,
  Cling to gilded toys of dust,
Boast of wealth, and fame, and pleasure:
  Only Jesus will I trust.
    Only Jesus! only Jesus!
    Only Jesus will I trust.

4 Since my eyes were fixed on Jesus,
  I've lost sight of all beside,—
So enchained my spirit's vision,
  Looking at the crucified.
    All for Jesus! all for Jesus!
    All for Jesus crucified!

5 Oh, what wonder! how amazing!
  Jesus, glorious King of kings,
Deigns to call me his beloved,
  Lets me rest beneath his wings.
    All for Jesus! all for Jesus!
    Resting now beneath his wings.

Cleansing Fountain. C. M.

COWPER.

1. There is a fountain fill'd with blood Drawn from Im-man-uel's veins,

S.

And sin-ners plung'd be-neath that flood Lose all their guilty stains.

D.C. And sin-ners plung'd be-neath that flood Lose all their guilty stains.

Fine.

D.S.S.

Lose all their guil-ty stains, Lose all their guil-ty stains.

2 The dying thief rejoiced to see
   That fountain in his day;
   And there have I, as vile as he,
   Wash'd all my sins away.

3 Dear dying Lamb, thy precious blood
   Shall never lose its power,
   Till all the ransom'd Church of God
   Be saved, to sin no more.

4 E'er since by faith I saw the stream
   Thy flowing wounds supply,
   Redeeming love has been my theme,
   And shall be till I die.

5 Then in a nobler, sweeter song,
   I'll sing thy power to save,
   When this poor lisping, stam'ring tongue
   Lies silent in the grave.

3

LONGING TO BE DISSOLVED IN LOVE.

1 Jesus hath died that I might live,
   Might live to God alone;
   In him eternal life receive,
   And be in spirit one.

2 Saviour, I thank thee for the grace,
   The gift unspeakable:
   And wait with arms of faith t'embrace,
   And all thy love to feel.

3 My soul breaks out in strong desire
   The perfect bliss to prove;
   My longing heart is all on fire
   To be dissolved in love.

4 Give me thyself: from every boast,
   From every wish set free;
   Let all I am in thee be lost,
   But give thyself to me.

5 Thy gifts, alas! cannot suffice,
   Unless thyself be given;
   Thy presence makes my paradise,
   And where thou art is heaven.

Gathering Jewels.

Miss P. J. Owens. W. J. Kirkpatrick. By per.

1. Jew - el-gatherers for a crown, Know ye not that many a gem,
2. Souls for whom the Saviour died, Souls enwrapp'd in sin-ful night,
3. Gems by cru - el hands de-faced, Pearls in heathen shadows dim,
4. With his blood wash'd white and pure, Gra - ven with his name di - vine,
5. Then our work shall be com-plete, Then we'll lay our offerings down,

Now in darkness trampled down, Might be-deck a di - a - dem.
Go and seek them far and wide, They will glit-ter in his sight.
Brilliants scatter'd in the waste, We must gather up for him.
These our jew-els shall en - dure, When the stars shall cease to shine.
We will lay them at his feet, He will lift them to his crown.

REFRAIN.

Gathering jewels, precious jewels, Blood-bought souls we seek to bring:

Gathering jewels, precious jewels, For the crown of Christ our King.

5   Entire Consecration.

Words by Frances Ridley Havergal.   Music by W. J. Kirkpatrick. By per.

1. Take my life, and let it be   Con - se - cra-ted, Lord, to thee;
2. Take my feet, and let them be   Swift and beau-ti - ful for thee;
3. Take my lips, and let them be   Fill'd with mes-sa - ges from thee;
4. Take my will, and make it thine;   It shall be no long-er mine;
5. Take my love—my Lord, I pour   At thy feet its treasure - store!

Take my hands, and let them move   At the im-pulse of thy love.
Take my voice, and let me sing   Al-ways, on - ly for my King.
Take my moments and my days;   Let them flow in ceaseless praise.
Take my heart—it is thine own,   It shall be thy roy - al throne.
Take my - self, and I will be   Ev - er, on - ly, all for thee!

CHORUS.

{ Wash me in the Saviour's precious blood, }
{ Cleanse me in its pu - ri - fy - ing flood; }   Lord, I give to thee my

life and all, to be   Thine, hence-forth, e - ter - nal - ly.

6 The Near To-morrow.

Words by SALLIE M. SMITH.

Music by JNO. R. SWENEY.

With feeling.

1. O, the changes, constant changes, In our pil-grim life be - low;
2. Here are bur-dens we must car - ry For our-selves and oth - ers too;
3. When our pil-grim life is end-ed, And we view the set - ting sun,

Chorus.—O, the near and bright to-mor-row: What a meeting will be ours,

Fine.

Through the sunshine and the shadow, Ev - er trusting, we must go:
But we have the Saviour's promise That our strength he will re-new.
When the la - bors of the har-vest We have finished one by one,

When we clasp our hands for - ev - er In a vale of songs and flow'rs.

But our faith be-holds the gleaming, And we hail the bless-ed ray
Thro' the man - y clouds that gath-er We can see the dawning ray
O, the rap - ture, ho - ly rap-ture; O, the shout of glad sur - prise,

D. C.

Of a near and bright to - mor-row That will nev - er pass a - way.
Of a near and bright to - mor-row That will nev - er pass a - way.
In the near and bright to - mor-row, When we ope our waking eyes.

Sinking out of Self.

Words by Rev. W. F. Crafts.

Music by Rev. R. Lowry.

From "Welcome Tidings," by per.

1. Now cru - ci - fied with Christ I am, The self with-in is slain;
2. Dead to the world and sin I am, A - live to God a - lone;
3. The throne of self with - in my heart, The King of saints does fill;
4. Here - af - ter, "it is no more I," Nor "sin" that ruleth me;

But still I live, and yet not I— Christ lives in me a - gain.
The life I have, I live by faith In God's be-lov - ed Son.
My spir - it crowns him Lord of all, And waits to do his will.
Reign, reign for - ev - er, blessed Christ, My all I give to thee.

CHORUS.

I am sinking out of self, out of self, into Christ, Sinking out of self into Christ.

I am sinking, sinking, sinking out of self, Sinking out of self in-to Christ.

Redeemed.

Words by FANNY J. CROSBY.   Music by W. J. KIRKPATRICK.   By per.

1. Redeem'd, how I love to proclaim it, Redeem'd by the blood of the Lamb ;
2. Redeem'd, and so happy in Je-sus, No language my rapture can tell ;
3. I think of my blessed Redeemer, I think of him all the day long ;
4. I know I shall see in his beauty, The King in whose law I de - light ;
5. I know there's a crown that is waiting In yonder bright mansion for me ;

Redeem'd thro' his infi ite mer - cy, His child and forever I am.
I know that the light of his presence With me doth continually dwell.
I sing, for I cannot be si - lent, His love is the theme of my song.
Who lovingly guardeth my footsteps, And giveth me songs in the night.
And soon with the spirits made perfect, At home with the Lord I shall be.

REFRAIN.

Re - deem'd, Re-deem'd, Redeem'd by the blood of the Lamb:
Redeem'd, Redeem'd,

Re - deem'd, Re-deem'd, His child and for - ev - er I am.
Redeem'd, Redeem'd,

From "SONGS OF TRIUMPH."

Jesus, my Joy.

Words by Mrs. J. F. CREWDSON.   Music by W. J. KIRKPATRICK. By per.

1. I've found a joy in sor-row, A se-cret balm for pain,
2. I've found a branch for heal-ing, Near every bit-ter spring,
3. I've found a glad ho-san-na For every woe and wail,
4. I've found the Rock of A-ges, When desert wells are dry;
5. An E-lim with its cool-ness, Its fountains and its shade;
6. O'er tears of soft con-tri-tion I've seen a rain-bow light:

A beau-ti-ful to-mor-row Of sun-shine af-ter rain.
A whis-per'd prom-ise steal-ing O'er ev-'ry bro-ken string.
A hand-ful of sweet man-na, When grapes of Eschol fail.
And af-ter wea-ry sta-ges, I've found an Elim nigh.
A bless-ing in its ful-ness, When buds of promise fade.
A glo-ry and fru-i-tion, So near! yet out of sight.

CHORUS.

'Tis Jesus, my portion for-ev-er, 'Tis Jesus, the First and the Last;

A help very present in trouble, A shelter from ev-'ry blast.

10   Return, O Return.

Words by LIZZIE EDWARDS.   Music by JNO. R. SWENEY.

1. There's a kind, gen-tle voice, full of pit-y and love; We hear its soft
2. There's a kind, pa-tient friend, who is pleading with you; The gift of his
3. There's a time drawing near when the voice you re-fuse No more will en-

whis-per wherev-er we move: How it speaks to the hearts that are
mer-cy he of-fers a-new: Ere the life-lamp shall cease in its
treat you sal-va-tion to choose: When the kind, patient friend, that so

S.   *Fine.*

wea-ry and worn—To Je-sus, who loves you, re-turn, O re-turn.
brightness to burn, Come quickly to Je-sus; re-turn, O re-turn.
cold-ly you spurn, Will call you no long-er; re-turn, O re-turn.

D.S. Je-sus, who loves you; re-turn, O re-turn.

CHORUS.

Return, O return, for why will ye stay? There's no oth-er refuge, there's

D.S.

no oth-er way: Come to him, O come to him, ye wea-ry and worn,—To

11   The Lily of the Valley.

As Sung by EDWARD E. NICKERSON.   Arr. by JOSHUA GILL.

1. I've found a friend in Jesus, he's everything to me,   He's the fair-est of ten
2. He all my griefs has taken, and all my sorrows borne ; In temptation he's my
3. He'll never, never leave me, nor yet forsake me here,   While I live by faith and

thousand to my soul ; The   Lily   of the Valley in him a-lone I   see,   All I
strong and mighty tow'r ; I've all for him forsaken, I've all my idols torn From my
do   his blessed will ;   A   wall of fire about me, I've nothing now to fear : With his

need to cleanse and make me fully whole. In sorrow he's my comfort, in trouble he's my
heart, and now he keeps me by his pow'r. Tho' all the world forsake me, and Satan tempts
man - na he my hungry soul shall fill ; Then sweeping up to glory we see his blessed

Chorus.—In sorrow he's my comfort, in trouble he's my

stay,   He   tells me   ev -'ry   care on him to roll. He's the Li-ly of the
sore, Through Je-sus   I   shall safe-ly reach the goal. He's the Li-ly of the
face, Where riv-ers   of   de-light shall ev - er   roll. He's the Li-ly of the

Hallelujah!

stay, He tells me ev -'ry care on him to roll. He's the Li-ly of the

D.S.

Valley, the bright and morning Star, He's the fairest of ten thousand to my soul.

Valley, the bright and morning Star, He's the fairest of ten thousand to my soul.

Thyself Instead.

Words by SALLIE M. SMITH.

Music by JNO. R. SWENEY.

1. Lord, take my heart, my wand'ring heart, To thee its pow'rs be-long;
2. Take from my soul its dross, re - fine, Its ev - 'ry sin re-move;
3. Take thou my days and let my hours Be spent a - lone for thee;
4. And when be - fore thy throne I stand, My toil and la - bor o'er,

Cast out each thought of un - be - lief, And fill me now with song.
Cast out the i - dols I have made, And fill me with thy love.
O give me strength my cross to bear, Whate'er that cross may be.
I'll strike the harp thy hand has tun'd, And praise thee ev - er-more.

CHORUS.

Since thou to pur-chase life for me Thy precious blood hast shed,

Take all I have for - ev - er dear, But give thy - self in-stead.

13   Saviour, Blessed Saviour.

Words by FANNY J. CROSBY.   Music by JNO. R. SWENEY.

1. O the joy, the bliss di-vine, Saviour, bless-ed Saviour,
2. Once my path was dark as night, Saviour, bless-ed Saviour,
3. Thou did'st give thy life for me, Saviour, bless-ed Saviour,
4. Make me strong-er, day by day, Saviour, bless-ed Saviour,

Thus to know and call thee mine, Saviour, bless-ed Sav-iour.
Now thy presence makes it bright, Saviour, bless-ed Sav-iour.
Now I give my all to thee, Saviour, bless-ed Sav-iour.
Still to run the heav'nly way, Saviour, bless-ed Sav-iour.

CHORUS.

Not a sor-row, not a care, Thou dost all my bur-dens bear,

While thy con-stant love I share, Sav-iour, bless-ed Sav-iour.

Happy in Jesus.

Words by FANNY J. CROSBY.　　　　　　　　　　Music by WM. J. KIRKPATRICK.

1. Hap - py in Jesus, happy in Je - sus, I will declare it a-broad;
2. Cling-ing to Jesus, on-ly to Je - sus, O what a comfort is mine;
3. Walk-ing with Jesus, on-ly with Je-sus, Sweetly I journey a-long;

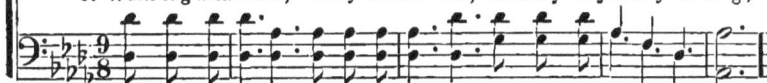

Cho.—Hap-py in Je-sus, happy in Je - sus, I will declare it a - broad;

Thro' his atonement, precious atonement, I have found favor with God.
I will a-dore him, yes, I will praise him, Je - sus, my Saviour di-vine.
I have believ'd him, I have receiv'd him, He is my joy and my song.

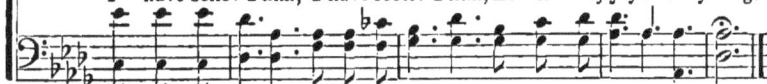

Thro' his atonement, precious atonement, I have found favor with God.

Kind-ly he sought me, tenderly brought me Out of the desert so wild:
Un - der his watchcare peacefully hiding, Faith my Redeemer can see;
Watching me ev-er, leaving me nev-er, Still my protector is nigh;

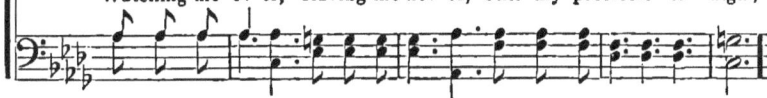

Now I can trust him, thankfully trust him, Since he has made me his child.
An - gels in glo-ry, telling the sto - ry, Now are re-joic-ing with me.
Sav'd by his mercy, in-fi-nite mer-cy, Who is so happy as I?

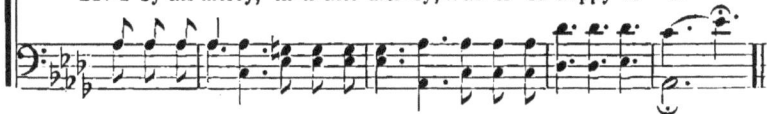

Wrestling Jacob.

Word. by Rev. CHARLES WESLEY.   Arr. by Rev. W. McDONALD.

1. { Come, O thou trav-el-ler unknown, Whom still I hold, but can-not see; }
{ My com-pa-ny be-fore is gone, And I am left a-lone with thee. }

With thee all night I mean to stay, And wrestle till the break of day, break of day.

2
I need not tell thee who I am:
My sin and misery declare;
Thyself hast called me by my name;
Look on thy hands, and read it there;
But who, I ask thee, who art thou?
Tell me thy name, and tell me now.

3
In vain thou strugglest to get free;
I never will unloose my hold:
Art thou the Man that died for me?
The secret of thy love unfold:
Wrestling, I will not let thee go,
Till I thy name, thy nature know.

4
Wilt thou not yet to me reveal
Thy new, unutterable name?
Tell me, I still beseech thee, tell;
To know it now resolved I am:
Wrestling, I will not let thee go,
Till I thy name, thy nature know.

5
What tho' my shrinking flesh complain,
And murmur to contend so long?
I rise superior to my pain:
When I am weak, then I am strong;
And when my all of strength shall fail,
I shall with the God-man prevail.

---

16   VICTORIOUS PRAYER.

1
Yield to me now, for I am weak,
But confident in self-despair;
Speak to my heart, in blessing, speak;
Be conquer'd by my instant prayer;
Speak, or thou never hence shalt move,
And tell me if thy name be Love?

2
'Tis Love! 'tis Love! thou di'dst for me;
I hear thy whisper in my heart;
The morning breaks, the shadows flee;
Pure, universal Love thou art:
To me, to all, thy bowels move,—
Thy nature and thy name is Love.

3
My prayer has pow'r with God; the grace
Unspeakable I now receive;
Through faith I see thee face to face;
I see thee face to face, and live!
In vain I have not wept and strove;
Thy nature and thy name is Love.

4
I know thee, Saviour, who thou art,—
Jesus, the feeble sinner's friend;
Nor wilt thou with the night depart,
But stay and love me to the end:
Thy mercies never shall remove;
Thy nature and thy name is Love.

17 Trust in Me.

Words by LIZZIE EDWARDS.

Music by JNO. R. SWENEY.

1. When my strength had well nigh fled, And my hope had died a - way,
2. When my bark, with shatter'd sail, Tried to meet the roll-ing wave,
3. Bless - ed Lord, that voice was thine; Still its lov-ing tones I hear,
4. Pre - cious words, that gave me rest, Sweeter far than all be - side,

Came a lov-ing voice that said— "Be not faithless, watch and pray."
Then that voice, a - mid the gale, Whisper'd "Lo I come to save."
Breathing life and peace di - vine In the precious word so dear.
Heal my wea-ry wounded breast, Taught me where my faith to hide.

CHORUS.

Trust in me, trust in me, I have suffer'd all for thee;
trust in me, trust in me, all for thee:

As thy day,.... thy strength shall be, I have promis'd, trust in me.
As thy day, thy strength shall be, strength shall be, trust in me.

As thy day,..... thy strength shall be,

As thy day, as thy day thy strength shall be, strength shall be, I have promis'd, trust in me

18   All in All to Me.

Words by FANNY J. CROSBY.   Music by WM. J. KIRKPATRICK.

1. Thou whose kind pro - tect-ing hand Leads me through a des - ert land,
2. Bless - ed Lord and Sav-iour mine, Hide my heart and keep it thine;
3. Lean - ing sweet-ly on thy breast, Let me still a - bide and rest;
4. When from earth my spir - it flies, Cloth'd in light be - yond the skies,

Source of love, I cling to thee, Thou art all in all to me.
Who, oh, who can love like thee, Thou art all in all to me.
On - ly there my soul would be, Thou art all in all to me.
This my song of praise will be, Thou art all in all to me.

CHORUS.

All to me, all to me, Thou art all in all to me;

Source of love, I cling to thee, Thou art all in all to me.

19   Rest for the Weary.

Words by Rev. S. G. HARMER.   Music by Rev. W. McDONALD.

1. In the Christian's home in glo-ry, There re - mains a land of rest;

2. Pain and sick-ness ne'er shall en - ter, Grief nor woe my lot shall share;

3. Death it - self shall then be vanquish'd, And his sting shall be withdrawn:

4. Sing, O sing, ye heirs of glo-ry; Shout your tri - umph as you go;

There my Saviour's gone be - fore me, To ful - fil my soul's re - quest.

But in that ce - lestial cen-tre, I a crown of life shall wear.

Shout for glad-ness, O ye ransom'd! Hail with joy the ris - ing morn.

Zi - on's gates will o - pen for you, You shall find an entrance through.

CHORUS.

There is rest for the wea - ry, There is rest for the

On the oth - er side of Jor - dan, In the sweet fields of

wea-ry, There is rest for the wea-ry, There is rest for you —

E - den, Where the tree of life is blooming, There is rest for you.

20   'Tis so Sweet to Trust in Jesus.

Words by Mrs. LOUISA M. R. STEAD.   Music by W. J. KIRKPATRICK. By per.

1. 'Tis so sweet to trust in Je-sus, Just to take him at his word;
2. O, how sweet to trust in Je-sus, Just to trust his cleansing blood;
3. Yes, 'tis sweet to trust in Je-sus, Just from sin and self to cease;
4. I'm so glad I learn'd to trust thee, Precious Je-sus, Saviour, Friend;

Just to rest up-on his promise; Just to know, "Thus saith the Lord."
Just in sim-ple faith to plunge me 'Neath the healing, cleansing flood.
Just from Je-sus sim-ply taking Life, and rest, and joy and peace.
And I know that thou art with me, Wilt be with me to the end.

REFRAIN.

Je-sus, Je-sus, how I trust him; How I've prov'd him o'er and o'er.

p

Je-sus, Je-sus, Precious Je-sus! O for grace to trust him more.

From "SONGS OF TRIUMPH."

And Can It Be?

Arranged by WM. G. FISCHER.

1. And can it be that I should gain An int'rest in the Saviour's blood?
Died he for me, who caus'd his pain? For me, who him to death pur - sued?

D.C. A - mazing love! how can it be, That thou, my Lord, shouldst die for me?

A - maz-ing love! how can it be, That thou, my Lord, shouldst die for me?

2
'Tis myst'ry all: th' Immortal dies!
  Who can explore his strange design?
In vain the first-born seraph tries
  To sound the depths of love divine.
'Tis mercy all! let earth adore;
Let angel minds inquire no more.

3
He left his Father's throne above;
  (So free, so infinite his grace!)
Emptied himself of all but love,
  And bled for Adam's helpless race.
'Tis mercy all, immense and free,
For O, my God, it found out me!

4
Long my imprison'd spirit lay,
  Fast bound in sin and nature's night;
Thine eye diffused a quickening ray;
  I woke; the dungeon flam'd with light;
My chains fell off, my heart was free—
I rose, went forth, and follow'd thee.

5
No condemnation now I dread;
  Jesus, with all in him, is mine;
Alive in him my living Head,
  And cloth'd in right'ousness divine,
Bold I approach th' eternal throne,
And claim the crown thro' Christ my own.

---

22   BELIEVING AGAINST HOPE.

1 Away, my unbelieving fear!
    Fear shall in me no more have place;
  My Saviour doth not yet appear—
    He hides the brightness of his face;
  But shall I therefore let him go,
    And basely to the tempter yield?
  No, in the strength of Jesus, no,
    I never will give up my shield.

2 Although the vine its fruit deny,
    Although the olive yield no oil,
  The with'ring fig trees droop and die,
    The field's elude the tiller's toil:

  The empty stall no herd afford,
    And perish all the bleating race;
  Yet will I triumph in the Lord,
    The God of my salvation praise.

3 In hope, believing against hope,
    Jesus, my Lord, my God I claim;
  Jesus, my strength, shall lift me up;
    Salvation is in Jesus' name;
  To me he soon shall bring it nigh;
    My soul shall then outstrip the wind;
  On wings of love mount up on high,
    And leave the world and sin behind.

23   It is Good to be Here.

Words by Rev. ISAAC N. WILSON.   Music by JNO. R. SWENEY. By per.

1. { While we bow in thy name, O   meet us a-gain;   Fill our
   { May the Spir-it of grace, and the smiles of thy face,   Gent-ly
2. { Our souls long for thee; O   may we now see   A
   { And feel as it rolls in   pow'r o'er our souls,   It is
3. { Thou art with us, we know; we   feel the sweet flow   Of the
   { We are wash'd from our sin, made all ho-ly with-in,   And in

D.S. light streaming down makes the path-way all clear: It is

REFRAIN.

Fine.

hearts with the light of thy love. }
fall on us now from a-bove. }   It is good to be here, It is
sin-cleansing blood wave ap-pear; }
good for us, Lord, to be here. }
sin-cleansing wave's gladd'ning tide; }
Je-sus we sweet-ly a-bide. }

good for us, Lord, to be here.

D. S.

good to be here; Thy per-fect love now drives a-way all our fear, And

Copyright, 1879, by Jno. R. SWENEY.

---

24   O HOW HAPPY ARE THEY.

1 O how happy are they
Who the Saviour obey,
And have laid up their treasures above;
Tongue can never express
The sweet comfort and peace
Of a soul in its earliest love.

2 That sweet comfort was mine,
When the favor divine
I received through the blood of the Lamb;
When my heart first believed,
What a joy I received—
What a heaven in Jesus' name!

3 'Twas a heaven below,
My Redeemer to know;
And the angels could do nothing more
Than to fall at his feet,
And the story repeat,
And the Lover of sinners adore.

4 Jesus, all the day long,
Was my joy and my song;
O, that all his salvation might see:
He hath loved me, I cried,
He hath suffered and died,
To redeem even rebels like me.

(22)

Redeemed and Washed.

Words by Rev. W. McDonald.   Arr. by Rev. W. McDonald.

1. Je - sus, Lord, I come to thee, Wash'd in the blood of the Lamb!
2. Speak, and let my heart be clean, Wash'd in the blood of the Lamb!
3. Cleanse me, wash me white as snow, Wash'd in the blood of the Lamb!
4. To my heart the bliss re - veal, Wash'd in the blood of the Lamb!
5. All thy full - ness now I claim, Wash'd in the blood of the Lamb!
6. I am sav'd by blood di - vine, Wash'd in the blood of the Lamb!

Set my long - ing spir - it free, Wash'd in the blood of the Lamb!
Ful - ly sav'd from in - bred sin, Wash'd in the blood of the Lamb!
Let me all thy full-ness know, Wash'd in the blood of the Lamb!
Fix on me the Spir-it's seal, Wash'd in the blood of the Lamb!
Thro' the dear Re-deem-er's name, Wash'd in the blood of the Lamb!
All the bliss of faith is mine, Wash'd in the blood of the Lamb!

CHORUS.

I'm re - deem'd, re - deem'd, Wash'd in the blood of the Lamb!

I'm re-deem'd, re - deem'd, I am wash'd in the blood of the Lamb!

26 More Like Thee.

W. J. K.   Music by W. J. KIRKPATRICK. By per.

1. Je - sus, Saviour, great Ex-am-ple,   Pat - tern of all pu - ri - ty,
2. Lest I wan-der from thy pathway,   Or my feet move wea - ri - ly,
3. When temptations fierce-ly lower,   And my shrinking soul would flee,
4. When a-round me all is darkness,   And thy beauties none may see,
5. When death's cold, repulsive fin-ger,   Leaves its im-press on my brow,

I would fol - low in thy footsteps, Dai - ly growing more like thee.
Sav - iour, take my hand and lead me; Keep me steadfast: more like thee.
Change each weakness in - to pow-er, Keep me spotless: more like thee.
May thy beams, O Glorious Brightness, In ef - ful-gence shine thro' me.
May thy life, with-in me swelling, Keep me sing-ing then as now.

REFRAIN.

More like thee, More like thee, Saviour, this my constant pray'r shall be:
More like thee, More like thee,

Day by day, where'er I stay, Make me more and more like thee.

27 The Love that Rescued Me.

Words by ETTA CLOUD.

Music by JNO. R. SWENEY. By per.

1. Lord, I come, I wait no long-er; Lo! I give my-self to thee:
2. Let me tell the wondrous sto-ry; Let me tell of Cal-va-ry;
3. See! the cru-el nails are driven Thro' the Saviour's hands and feet;
4. Yes, the sac-ri-fice is offer'd, Life is bought for you and me;
5. In my heart hope's star is shining With a ra-diance from a-bove,

Thou hast fin-ish'd my redemption; Thou hast res-cued e-ven me.
Of the won-der-ful compassion That could res-cue e-ven me.
See him dy-ing! hear him saying, "All is finish'd," 'tis com-plete.
Lord, I come, I wait no longer, Lo! I give my-self to thee.
And my soul is sweet-ly resting In the o-cean of thy love.

REFRAIN.

O, the mer-cy so a-mazing; O, the grace so full and free;

O, the love so strong and boundless, That could rescue e-ven me.

Copyright, 1882, by Jno. R. SWENEY.

Companionship with Jesus.

Words by Mary D. James. Music by W. J. Kirkpatrick. By per.

1. Oh, bles - sed fel - low-ship divine! Oh, joy supremely sweet! Com-
2. I'm walk-ing close to Je-sus' side; So close that I can hear The
3. I'm lean-ing on his loving breast, A-long life's weary way; My
4. I know his shelt'ring wings of love Are al-ways o'er me spread; And

pan - ion-ship with Je - sus here Makes life with bliss re - plete: In
soft - est whispers of his love In fel - low-ship so dear, And
path, il - lumined by his smiles, Grows brighter day by day: No
though the storms may fiercely rage, All calm and free from dread, My

un - ion with the pur - est one, I find my heav'n on earth be-gun.
feel his great Al-might-y hand Protects me in this hostile land.
foes, no woes my heart can fear, With my Al-might-y Friend so near.
peace-ful spir - it ev - er sings "I'll trust the cov-ert of thy wings.

REFRAIN.

Oh, wondrous bliss! oh, joy sublime! I've Je - sus with me all the time!

Oh, wondrous bliss! oh, joy sublime! I've Je - sus with me all the time!

29 Follow Me.

Words by Rev. G. D. WATSON, D. D.   Music arranged for this Work.

1. I hear my dy - ing Sav-iour say, Fol-low me, come, fol - low me;
2. I know thy life of guilt and pain, Fol-low me, come, fol - low me;
3. Tho' thou hast sinn'd, I'll pardon thee, Fol-low me, come, fol - low me;

His voice is call - ing all the day, Fol-low me, come, fol-low me.
I know each ache of heart and brain, Fol-low me, come, fol-low me.
From in-bred sin I'll set thee free, Fol-low me, come, fol-low me.

For thee I tread the bit-ter way, For thee I give my life a-way,
For thee I left my heav'nly train, For thee I've open'd ev - 'ry vein,
In all thy changing life I'll be Thy God, and guide o'er land and sea,

And drink the gall thy debt to pay, Fol-low me, come, fol - low me.
And now I plead yet once a - gain, Fol-low me, come, fol - low me.
Thy bliss thro' all e - ter - ni - ty, Fol-low me, come, fol - low me.

4 Come cast upon me all thy cares,
   Follow me, come, follow me;
Thy heavy load my arm upbears,
   Follow me, come, follow me.
Lean on my breast, dismiss thy fears,
And trust me through the future years,
My hand shall wipe away thy tears,
   Follow me, come, follow me.

5 Dear Lord, I yield to all thy will,
   I'll follow thee, yes, follow thee;
O! bid my struggling soul be still,
   I'll follow thee, yes, follow thee.
Come cleanse, and with thy Spirit fill,
And keep me safe from every ill,
And all thy word in me fulfil,
   I'll follow thee, yes, follow thee.

Melody used by permission of O. Ditson & Co.   *Copyright, 1885, by McDonald & Gill.*

30   Closer Walk with Thee.

Words by MARTHA J. LANKTON.   Music by WM. J. KIRKPATRICK.

Not too fast.

1. I am hap-py, O my Saviour, For I know that I am thine,
2. 'Tis thy hand, the clouds re-mov-ing, Scat-ters sunshine o'er my way;
3. To the heights of sa-cred rap-ture, That I nev-er yet have known,

Thro' the pure and per-fect cleansing Of thy precious blood di-vine:
I am feast-ing at the ban-quet Of thy mer-cy ev-'ry day:
Let me soar a-way in tri-umph, Till my faith shall touch thy throne:

But my soul would rise still high-er, There are great-er joys for me;
But my soul would drink more deeply At the Fount of Life so free:
In the wide unfathom'd o-cean Of thy mighty love so free,

I am long-ing, I am praying For a closer walk with thee.
O my Saviour, I am pleading For a closer walk with thee.
Let the ti-dal wave roll o'er me, Till my soul is lost in thee.

CHORUS.

1 & 2. For a closer walk with thee, For a closer walk with thee;
3.   Till my soul is lost in thee, Till my soul is lost in thee;

Closer Walk with Thee. Concluded.

Saviour, come, a - bide with me, I am long - - - ing,
I am longing, I am longing,

I am pray - - - ing For a closer walk with thee.
I am praying, I am praying

---

31 ## My Saviour.

Words by Dora Greenwell.   Music by Wm. J. Kirkpatrick

1. I am not skill'd to understand What God hath will'd, what God hath plann'd ;
2. I take God at his word and deed: "Christ died to save me," this I read,

I on - ly know at his right hand Stands One who is my Saviour.
And in my heart I find a need Of him to be my Saviour.

3 And was there, then, no other way
For God to take?—I cannot say ;
I only bless him, day by day,
Who saved me through my Saviour.

4 That he should leave his place on high
And come for sinful man to die,
You count it strange?—so do not I,
Since I have known my Saviour.

5 And oh! that he fulfilled may see
The travail of his soul in me,
And with his work contented be,
As I with my dear Saviour!

6 Yea, living, dying, let me bring
My strength, my solace from this spring,
That he who lives to be my King
Once died to be my Saviour!

32 When the Voyage is Ended.

Words by FANNY J. CROSBY.   Music by JNO. R. SWENEY. By per.

1. When the voyage of life is end-ed, And the stormy winds shall
2. When we gath - - - - er in the morning, And the long, long night is
3. O, the pearl - - - - y gates of glo - ry, Not a - jar, but o - pen
4. Hal-le-lu - - - - jah! hal-le-lu - jah! O, ye ransom'd hosts a -

When the

cease, When we step from care and sorrow To e - ter-nal joy and peace.
o'er, When we clasp our hands u - nit-ed, And our partings come no more.
wide, E - ven now our faith beholds them, As we near the swelling tide.
bove, We are com - - ing, we are coming, Soon we'll join your song of love.

When we

REFRAIN.

Hal - le - lu - jah, hal - le - lu - jah, what a meet - ing! But the

best of all will be, Our Re - deem - - -

But the best of all will be, Our Re - deemer, our Re -

er, dear Re-deem - er, In his beau-ty we shall see.

deem-er.

From "SONGS OF TRIUMPH."

30

33 My Spirit is Free.

W. A. S. Music by Rev. W. A. Spencer. By per.

1. I follow the footsteps of Jesus, my Lord, His Spirit doth lead me a-long;
2. A lep - er he found me, polluted by sin, From which he alone can set free;
3. A cap-tive in woe to my prison of night, The Master hath open'd the door;
4. Proclaim it, 'tis done, full salvation is wrought For sinners from sorrow and woe;

I walk in the pathway made plain by his word, And he fills all my soul with this song.
He spake, in his mercy, "I will, be thou clean," And he instantly pu-ri-fied me.
Shout aloud of deliv'rance, ye angels of light, Praise his name, O my soul, evermore.
Sing aloud of his grace who my pardon has bought, "For his blood washes whiter than
[snow."

CHORUS.

Glo - ry to God, my spirit is free, Glo-ry to God, he pu-ri-fies me;

I'm walking the thorn-path, but joyful I'll be While following Jesus, my Lord.

34 God's Anvil.

Words from the GERMAN.   Music by QUISQUAM.

1. Pain's furnace-heat within me quivers, God's breath upon the flame doth blow,
2. He comes and lays my heart all heated,   On his hard anvil, minded so;
3. He takes my soften'd heart and beats it; The sparks fly off at every   blow:
4. He kindles for my profit,   purely,   Affliction's glowing, fiery   brand:
5. I will not murmur at the sorrow   That only longer-liv'd would be:

And   all my heart in anguish shivers   And trembles at the fi - ery glow.
Yet   in his own fair form to beat it   With his great hammer, blow by blow.
He turns it o'er and o'er and heats it,   And let's it cool, and makes it glow.
For   all his heaviest blows are surely   In - flict-ed by a Mas-ter hand.
The end may come, and that to-morrow, When God hath wrought his will in me.

CHORUS.

And yet I whisper, "As God will," And in his hottest fire hold still.

And yet I whisper, "As God will," And in his hottest fire hold still.

35 I'm Saved!

Words by Rev. E. H Stokes, D. D. Music by Jno. A. Duncan. By per.

1. I'm sav'd! I'm sav'd! oh, blessed Lord, I'm sweet-ly sav'd in thee;
2. I'm sav'd! I'm sav'd! oh, joy sub-lime! I'm sav'd from self and sin;
3. Sav'd at the cross, the blessed cross; Sav'd without and with-in:
4. I'm sav'd! I'm sav'd! I'll tell it here, I'll sing it o'er and o'er;

Sav'd by thy blood and by thy word, And thine henceforth will be.
I'm sav'd, I'm sav'd, oh, bliss di-vine! And love has clos'd me in.
I'm sav'd, I'm sav'd, oh, what a loss Who fail this joy to win.
I'm sav'd in Je-sus, oh, how sweet! I'll sing it ev - er - more.

REFRAIN.

I'm sav'd! I'm sav'd! I'm sav'd! I'm wash'd in the blood of the Lamb.

I'm sav'd! I'm sav'd! I'm sav'd! I'm wash'd in the blood of the Lamb.

36 Is my Name Written There?

M. A. K. Music by FRANK M. DAVIS. By per.

1. Lord, I care not for rich-es, Neither silver nor gold; I would make sure of
2. Lord, my sins they are many, Like the sands of the sea; But thy blood, oh, my
3. Oh! that beautiful cit - y, With its mansions of light, With its glo-ri - fied

heav-en, I would en - ter the fold. In the book of thy kingdom, With its
Sav-iour! Is suf - fi - cient for me: For thy promise is written In bright
be - ings, In pure garments of white, Where no e - vil thing cometh, To de-

pa - ges so fair, Tell me, Je - sus, my Saviour, Is my name written there?
let-ters that glow, "Tho' your sins be as scarlet, I will make them like snow."
spoil what is fair; Where the angels are watching, Is my name written there?

REFRAIN.

Is my name writ - ten there, On the page white and fair?

In the book of thy king-dom, Is my name writ - ten there?

34

37 Watch and Pray.

Words by FANNY J. CROSBY.　　　　　　　　　　Music by W. J. KIRKPATRICK.

1. Watch and pray that when the Master cometh, If at morning, noon or night,
2. Watch and pray; the tempter may be near us; Keep the heart with jealous care,
3. Watch and pray, nor let us ev-er wea-ry; Je-sus watch'd and pray'd alone:
4. Watch and pray, nor leave our post of du-ty, Till we hear the Bridegroom's voice:

He may find a lamp in ev'ry window, Trimm'd and burning clear and bright.
Lest the door a moment left unguarded, E-vil thoughts may en-ter there.
Pray'd for us when only stars beheld Him, While on Olive's brow they shone.
Then with Him the marriage feast partaking, We shall ev-er-more re-joice.

CHORUS.

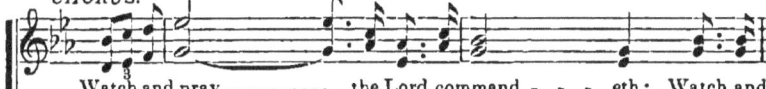

Watch and pray,.......... the Lord command - - - eth; Watch and

Watch and pray, the Lord commandeth, Watch and pray, the Lord commandeth; Watch [and

pray,........ 'twill not be long: Soon he'll gath - - -

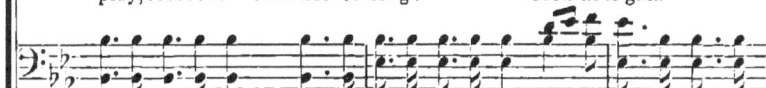

pray, 'twill not be long, Watch and pray, 'twill not be long : Soon he'll gather home his

- - - er home his lov'd ones To the hap-py vale of song. of song.
the happy vale of song.

lov'd ones, Soon he'll gather home his lov'd ones To the happy vale of song.

I Know Not Why!

Words by GRACIE E. LOVELIGHT.　　　　Music by WM. J. KIRKPATRICK.

1. I know not why my Saviour Has done so much for me;　I know not why his
2. I know not why my Saviour Should leave a glorious throne To bleed and die on
3. I know not why he bids me Breathe forth my wants in prayer, While day by day

[he

fa - vor Has come so constantly;　But this I know, I love him And
Calvary, For sin - ners to a - tone;　But this I know, 'tis cer-tain, He
sees me, And knows my ev-'ry care;　But this I know, while praying And

trust him day by day, And cast my care upon him, And watch and praise and pray.
ful - ly ransom'd me. And in that truth believing I re - al-ize I'm free.
trusting in his word, My soul refresh'd and strengthen'd Rests sweetly on the Lord.

4 I know not where he leads me,　　　But this I know, at duty,
　And yet I follow still;　　　　　　　In prayer or holy song,
I know not why he needs me　　　　My heart keeps overflowing
　My vineyard place to fill:　　　　　With rapture all day long!

39　PRECIOUS SAVIOUR, THOU HAST SAVED ME.
(No. 33 in "BEULAH SONGS.")

1 Precious Saviour, thou hast sav'd me;
　Thine and only thine I am;
Oh, the cleansing blood has reach'd me,
　Glory, glory to the Lamb!
　　Chorus.
Glory, glory, Jesus saves me,
　Glory, glory to the Lamb!
Oh, the cleansing blood has reach'd me,
　Glory, glory to the Lamb!

2 Long my yearning heart was trying
　To enjoy this perfect rest;
But I gave all trying over:
　Simply trusting, I was blest.

3 Trusting, trusting every moment;
　Feeling now the blood applied;　(36)

Lying at the cleansing fountain;
　Dwelling in my Saviour's side.

4 Consecrated to thy service,
　I will live and die to thee;
I will witness to thy glory
　Of salvation full and free.

5 Yes, I will stand up for Jesus;
　He has sweetly saved my soul,
Cleansed me from inbred corruption,
　Sanctified, and made me whole.

6 Glory to the blood that bought me,
　Glory to its cleansing power!
Glory to the blood that keeps me!
　Glory, glory evermore!

LOUISE M. ROUSE.

40   Bringing in the Sheaves.

Words from "Songs of Glory."   Music by Geo. A. Minor. By per.

1. Sowing in the morning, sowing seeds of kindness, Sowing in the noon-tide,
2. Sowing in the sunshine, sowing in the shadows, Fearing neither clouds nor
3. Go, then, ev - er weeping, sowing for the Master, Tho' the loss sustain'd our

and the dew - y eves; Waiting for the harvest, and the time of reaping,
winter's chilling breeze; By and by the harvest, and the la - bor ended,
spir - it oft - en grieves; When our weeping's over, he will bid us welcome,

REFRAIN.

We shall come re - joic-ing, bringing in the sheaves. Bringing in the sheaves,

bringing in the sheaves, We shall come re - joic-ing, bringing in the sheaves.

Bringing in the sheaves,   We shall come rejoicing,
   bringing in the sheaves,   [bringing in the sheaves.

41 What a Gath'ring that will be.

J. H. K.

Music by J. H. KURZENKNABE.

1. At the sounding of the trumpet, when the saints are gather'd home, We will
2. When the angel of the Lord proclaims that time shall be no more, We shall
3. At the great and final judgment, when the hidden comes to light, When the
4. When the golden harps are sounding, and the angel bands proclaim In tri -

greet each other by the crystal sea, With the friends and all the lov'd ones there a-
gather, and the sav'd and ransom'd see; Then to meet again together, on the
Lord in all his glory we shall see; At the bidding of our Saviour, "Come, ye
umphant strains the glorious jubilee; Then to meet and join to sing the song of

crystal sea,

wait-ing us to come, What a gath'ring of the faith-ful that will be!
bright ce - les-tial shore, What a gath'ring of the faith-ful that will be!
bless-ed, to my right," What a gath'ring of the faith-ful that will be!
Mo - ses and the Lamb, What a gath'ring of the faith-ful that will be!

CHORUS.

What a gath - - - 'ring, gath - - 'ring, At the
What a gath-'ring of the lov'd ones when we'll meet with one an - oth-er,

sounding of the glorious ju - bi - lee! What a gath - - 'ring
jubilee! What a gath'ring when the friends and all the

From "SONG TREASURY," by per. 38

What a Gath'ring, etc. Concluded.

gath - - - 'ring, What a gath'ring of the faith-ful that will be!
dear ones meet each oth-er,

---

42 Oh! 'tis Glory in My Soul.

Words by FLORA L. BEST. Music by JNO. R. SWENEY.

1. To thy cross, dear Christ, I'm clinging, All my re - fuge and my plea;
2. Long my heart hath heard thee call-ing, But I thrust a - side thy grace;
3. Love e - ter - nal, light e - ter - nal, Close me safe - ly, sweet-ly in;

Matchless is thy lov-ing kindness, Else it had not stoop'd to me.
Yet, O boundless con-de - scen-sion, Love is shin-ing from thy face.
Sav - iour, let thy balm of heal-ing Ev - er keep me free from sin.

CHORUS.

Oh, 'tis glo-ry! oh, 'tis glo-ry! Oh, 'tis glo - ry in my soul,

For I've touch'd the hem of his garment, And his pow'r doth make me whole.

By permission.

43   "Thine."

Words by Mrs. MARY D. JAMES.

Music by WM. J. KIRKPATRICK.

1. What bliss in - ef - fa - ble, di - vine, Is cen - ter'd in that
2. Tho' oft the bit - ter cup be giv'n, And crea - ture joys de -
3. What mat-ters then my earth-ly loss, And sore be - reave-ments
4. The tempter's pow'r can nev - er harm, While Je - sus is so
5. No earthly claim, no mor - tal love, My heart from thee shall

word! To know and feel that I am Thine, My liv - ing, lov - ing Lord!
part; Tho' fondest earth - ly ties be riv'n, And anguish rend the heart,
here? What tho' I bear a heav-y cross, With many a fall - ing tear?
near; Nor darkest cloud, nor hardest storm Can move my heart with fear,
call, For all my be - ing's pow-ers move To thee, my Christ, my All!

What joy su - preme - ly sweet is mine—To say, dear Je - sus, I am Thine!
Thy smiles bring com-fort so be-nign,—And joyous-ly I say I'm Thine!
A glorious re - compense is mine—For I can say, dear Lord, I'm Thine!
While on thy bo - som I re-cline, And feel that I am wholly Thine!
In ev - er - last - ing bonds di-vine, Je-sus—my Lord, I'm wholly Thine!

CHORUS.

En-tire-ly Thine, for-ev-er Thine, My own Re - deem-er, on - ly Thine!

44 Keep me Ever.

Words by SALLIE M. SMITH.   Music by JNO. R. SWENEY.

1. In thy per - fect peace di - vine, Keep, O keep me ev - er;
2. At my post of du - ty still Keep, O keep me ev - er;
3. 'Neath thy all pro - tect-ing wings, Keep, O keep me ev - er;
4. Till my last ex - pir-ing breath, Keep, O keep me ev - er;

Where my faith will brightest shine, Keep, O keep me ev - er.
Learn - ing there thy righteous will, Keep, O keep me ev - er.
By the soul re-fresh-ing springs, Keep, O keep me ev - er.
Thine in life, and thine in death, Keep, O keep me ev - er.

CHORUS.

Let thy heart my dwelling be, Let thy word a - bide in me;

In the path that leads to thee, Keep, O keep me ev - er.

45 Welcome for Me.

Words by Fanny J. Crosby.
Music by Wm. J. Kirkpatrick.

1. Like a bird on the deep, far a-way from its nest, I had
2. I am safe in the ark; I have fold-ed my wings On the
3. I am safe in the ark, and I dread not the storm, Tho' a-

wander'd, my Saviour, from thee; But thy dear lov-ing voice call'd me
bo-som of mer-cy di-vine; I am fill'd with the light of thy
round me the surges may roll; I will look to the skies, where the

home to thy breast, And I knew there was welcome for me.
presence so bright, And the joy that will ev-er be mine.
day nev-er dies, I will sing of the joy in my soul.

CHORUS.

Welcome for me, Saviour from thee; A smile and a welcome for me:

Now, like a dove, I rest in thy love, And find a sweet refuge in thee.
In thee.

46 Mighty to Save.

Words by Rev. R. W. Todd.   Music by Harry Sanders. By per.

1. O who is this that cometh From Edom's crimson plain, With wounded side, with garments dy'd? O tell me now thy name. "I that saw thy soul's distress, A ran - som gave; I, that speak in righteousness, Mighty to save."

REFRAIN.

Mighty to save,...   Mighty to save,...

Mighty to save,   Mighty to save,

Mighty to save, Lord, I trust thy wondrous love, Mighty to save.

2 O why is thine apparel
  With reeking gore all dyed,
Like them that tread the wine-press red?
  O why this bloody tide?
"I the wine-press trod alone,
  'Neath darkening skies;
Of the people there was none
  Mighty to save."

3 O, bleeding Lamb, my Saviour,
  How couldst thou bear this shame?
"With mercy fraught, mine own arm bro't
  Salvation in my name:
I the bloody fight have won,
  Conquered the grave;
Now the year of joy has come,
  Mighty to save."

47 The Rock that is Higher than I.

Words by E. JOHNSON. Music by WM. G. FISCHER. By per.

1. Oh, sometimes the shad-ows are deep, And rough seems the path to the goal;
2. Oh, sometimes how long seems the day, And sometimes how weary my feet;
3. Oh, near to the Rock let me keep, Or blessings, or sor-rows pre-vail;

And sorrows, sometimes how they sweep Like tempests down o-ver the soul.
But, toil - ing in life's dusty way, The Rock's blessed shadow, how sweet!
Or climbing the mountain way steep, Or walk-ing the shadow - y vale.

CHORUS.

Oh, then to the Rock let me fly, To the
let me fly,

Rock that is high-er than I; Oh, then to the Rock let me
is higher than I;

fly, To the Rock that is high - er than I.
let me fly,

48   Shall we all be there?

Words by FANNY J. CROSBY.　　　　　　　　Music by JNO. R. SWENEY.

1. Are we all safe in Je-sus? Is it well with ev-'ry soul? Have we
2. Are we all safe in Je-sus? Is our anchor firm and strong, And our
3. Are we all safe in Je-sus? Is there one outside the fold Who re-

been to the fountain? Has its cleansing made us whole? Are we all safe in
hope looking upward With a cheerful, hap-py song? In the life-work be-
gards not the sto-ry That so oft has here been told? Still for you there is

Je-sus? Are we trust-ing him a-lone? Is it joy, is it rap-ture,
fore us, Thro' the tri-als that may come, Can we cling to the promise,
mer-cy, To the Sav-iour quickly fly: Do not wait, do not tar-ry,

CHORUS.

Thus to gath-er at his throne? On the bright, bright hills of glory, In our
There is bless-ed rest at home?
For he now is pass-ing by!

Father's mansion fair, When the faithful ones are gather'd, Shall we all, all be there?

Copyright, 1885, by Jno. R. SWENEY.

45

49. We Shall Know.

Words by ANNIE HERBERT. Music by J. H. ANDERSON.

1. When the mists have roll'd in splen-dor From the beau-ty of the hills,
2. If we err, in hu-man blindness, And for-get that we are dust;
3. When the mists have ris'n a-bove us, As our Father knows his own,

And the sunshine, warm and ten-der, Falls in kiss-es on the rills,
If we miss the law of kindness When we struggle to be just,
Face to face with those that love us, We shall know as we are known;

We may read love's shin-ing let-ter In the rain-bow of the spray:
Snow-y wings of peace shall cov-er All the plain that hides a-way,
Love, be-yond the o-rient meadows Floats the gold-en fringe of day,

We shall know each oth-er bet-ter When the mists have clear'd a-way.
When the wea-ry watch is o-ver, And the mists have clear'd a-way.
Heart to heart we bide the shadows, Till the mists have clear'd a-way.

We Shall Know. Concluded.

We shall know.... as we are known,.. Nev-er-more.... to walk a-

We shall know, as we are known, Nev-er-more

lone, In the dawn - - - ing of the morn-ing, When the

to walk a - lone, In the dawn-ing of the morn - ing,

mists.... have clear'd a-way; In the dawn - - ing of the

When the mists have clear'd a-way; In the dawning

morn-ing, When the mists........ have clear'd a - way.

When the mists have clear'd a - way.

47

50   At the Mercy-seat.

Words by E. CUTLER.

Music by WM. J. KIRKPATRICK

1. A - mid the toils and cares of life, A - mid the tur-moil and the strife,
2. In sore temptation's try-ing hour, When o'er the wi-ly tempter's pow'r
3. When darkness gathers round my way, And I can see no cheer-ing ray,
4. And when my path is bright and clear, Without a cloud of doubt or fear,

Rest to the wea-ry soul is sweet: I find it at the mer-cy - seat.
I strive for vic - to - ry com-plete, I gain it at the mer-cy - seat.
To guide my weary, falt -'ring feet, I tar-ry at the mer-cy - seat.
My heart is fill'd with peace so sweet, While waiting at the mer-cy - seat.

REFRAIN.

At the mer - - - - cy - seat, At the mer - - - - cy - seat:

At the mer-cy - seat,   At the mer-cy - seat:

I love to hold communion sweet With Jesus, at the mer-cy-seat.

51   Whosoever Believeth.

"For God so loved the world, that he gave his only begotten Son, that whosoever believeth in him should not perish, but have everlasting life."—John 3: 16.

Words by Rev. F. DENISON.   Music by W. WARREN BENTLEY. By per.

1. From Calvary's mountain sounding, What lov - ing words we hear;
2. Whoe'er my word be - liev - eth, We hear the Sav-iour say,
3. O, broth-er, come and trust him, O, come to him to - day;

The love of God a - bound-ing, Dis-pel - ling all our fear.
A par - don full re - ceiv - eth: All sins are wash'd a - way.
He's wait-ing to re - ceive you, Why long-er then de - lay.

REFRAIN.

Who - so - ev - er be - liev - eth, Who - so - ev - er be - liev - eth,

Who - so - ev - er be - liev - eth, Hath ev - er - last - ing life.

52   For You and for Me.

W. L. T.

Music by WILL L. THOMPSON.

Very slow. pp

1. Soft - ly and tenderly Je - sus is calling, Call-ing for you and for me;
2. Why should we tarry when Jesus is pleading, Pleading for you and for me?
3. Time is now fleeting, the moments are passing, Passing from you and from me;
4. Oh, for the wonderful love he has promis'd, Promis'd for you and for me;

See on the portals he's waiting and watching, Watching for you and for me.
Why should we linger and heed not his mercies, Mercies for you and for me?
Shadows are gathering, death beds are coming, Coming for you and for me.
Though we have sinn'd he has mercy and pardon, Pardon for you and for me.

m CHORUS.   *cres.*

Come home,   Come home;   Ye who are weary, come home....

Come home,   Come home,

pp   *ppp*   *rit.*

Earnestly, tenderly, Je - sus is calling, Calling, O sinner, come home!

53 Remembered by what I have done.

Words by Rev. H. Bonar, D. D.   Music by W. Warren Bentley. By per.

1. Up, and a - way, like the dew of the morning, Soaring from earth to its
2. Shall I be miss'd if an-oth-er succeed me, Reaping the fields I in
3. On - ly the truth that in life I have spoken, On - ly the seed that on
4. Oh, when the Saviour shall make up his jewels, When the bright crowns of re-

home in the sun; Thus would I pass from the earth and its toil-ing,
spring-time have sown? No, for the sow-er may pass from his la - bors,
earth I have sown; These shall pass onward when I am for-got-ten,
joic - ing are won; Then will his faith-ful and wea - ry dis - ci - ples,

REFRAIN.

On - ly remember'd by what I have done. On - ly remember'd,
On - ly remember'd by what he has done.
Fruits of the har-vest and what I have done.
All be remember'd for what they have done.

On - ly remember'd, On - ly remember'd by what I have done.

rit.

Only remember'd, On - ly remember'd, Only remember'd by what I have done.

54   Jesus Comes.

Words by Mrs. PHOEBE PALMER.   Music by WM. J. KIRKPATRICK.

1. Watch, ye saints, with eyelids waking, Lo, the pow'rs of heav'n are shaking;
2. Lo! the promise of your Saviour: Pardon'd sin and purchas'd fa - vor,
3. Kingdoms at their base are crumbling, Hark, his chariot wheels are rumbling;
4. Nations wane, tho' proud and stately, Christ his kingdom hasteneth greatly;
5. Lamb of God!—thou meek and lowly, Ju-dah's li - on!—high and ho - ly;
6. Sinners, come, while Christ is pleading, Now for you he's in - ter - ced-ing;

Keep your lamps all trimm'd and burning, Ready for your Lord's re-turn-ing.
Blood-wash'd robes and crowns of glory; Haste to tell redemption's sto - ry.
Tell, O, tell of grace abounding, Whilst the seventh trump is sounding.
Earth her la-test pangs is summing, Shout, ye saints, your Lord is coming.
Lo! thy Bride comes forth to meet thee, All in blood-wash'd robes to greet thee.
Haste, ere grace and time diminished Shall proclaim the mystery finished.

REFRAIN.

Lo! he comes, lo! Je-sus comes; Lo! he comes, he comes all glorious!

Je - sus comes to reign vic - to-rious, Lo! he comes, yes, Je-sus comes.

55. Are you Wash'd in the Blood?

Words and Music by Rev. ELISHA A. HOFFMAN.

1. Have you been to Je-sus for the cleansing pow'r? Are you wash'd in the
2. Are you walking dai-ly by the Saviour's side? Are you wash'd in the
3. When the Bridegroom cometh, will your robes be white, Pure and white in the
4. Lay a-side the garments that are stain'd with sin, And be wash'd in the

blood of the Lamb? Are you ful-ly trusting in his grace this hour? Are you
blood of the Lamb? Do you rest each moment in the Cru-ci-fied? Are you
blood of the Lamb? Will your soul be ready for the mansions bright, And be
blood of the Lamb? There's a fountain flowing for the soul unclean, O be

CHORUS.

wash'd in the blood of the Lamb? Are you wash'd in the
Are you wash'd

blood, In the soul-cleansing blood of the Lamb? Are your garments
In the blood, of the Lamb?

spotless? Are they white as snow? Are you wash'd in the blood of the Lamb?

From "SPIRITUAL SONGS," by permission.

53

56   I am Saved.

Words by Mrs. S. L. OBERHOLTZER.   Music by JNO. R. SWENEY.

1. I am sav'd! the Lord hath sav'd me, Help me shout the glorious news!
2. Loud I sing my ex-ul-ta-tion, Hoping it will reach the skies;
3. Free sal-va-tion! glad sal-va-tion! Let us shout from pole to pole,
4. When at last the days are gathered In-to thy great judgment one,

I have tast-ed God's sal-va-tion, And 'tis sweet as honeyed dews.
Keep, dear Lord, my soul for-ev-er Un-der thy pro-tect-ing eyes.
Un-til each dis-eas-ed na-tion Feels that God hath made it whole.
May I find my name deep written In the re-cords of thy Son.

CHORUS.

Glo-ry, glo-ry, hal-le-lu-jah! I re-joice sal-va-tion came;

Glo-ry, glo-ry, hal-le-lu-jah! I am sav'd in Je-sus' name.

57 Cross and Crown. C. M.

1. Must Je-sus bear the cross a-lone, And all the world go free?

No: there's a cross for every one, And there's a cross for me.

2 How happy are the saints above,
  Who once went sorrowing here;
  But now they taste unmingled love
  And joy without a tear.

3 The consecrated cross I'll bear,
  Till death shall set me free,
  And then go home my crown to wear,
  For there's a crown for me.

4 Upon the crystal pavement, down
  At Jesus' pierced feet,
  Joyful, I'll cast my golden crown,
  And his dear name repeat.

5 O precious cross! O glorious crown!
  O resurrection day!
  Ye angels, from the stars come down,
  And bear my soul away.

58 LET HIM TO WHOM WE NOW BELONG.

1 Let him to whom we now belong,
  His Sovereign right assert;
  And take up every thankful song
  And every loving heart.

2 He justly claims us for his own,
  Who bought us with a price;
  The Christian lives to Christ alone;
  To Christ alone he dies.

3 Jesus! thine own at last receive;
  Fulfil our hearts' desire;
  And let us to thy glory live,
  And in thy cause expire.

4 Our souls and bodies we resign;
  With joy we render thee
  Our all,—no longer ours, but thine
  To all eternity.

59 O FOR A HEART TO PRAISE MY GOD.

1 O for a heart to praise my God,
  A heart from sin set free;—
  A heart that always feels thy blood,
  So freely spilt for me!

2 A heart resign'd, submissive, meek,
  My great Redeemer's throne;
  Where only Christ is heard to speak,—
  Where Jesus reigns alone.

3 O for a lowly, contrite heart,
  Believing, true, and clean;
  Which neither life nor death can part
  From him that dwells within:—

4 A heart in every thought renew'd,
  And full of love Divine;
  Perfect and right, and pure and good,
  A copy, Lord, of thine.

60 COME, O MY GOD, THE PROMISE SEAL.

1 Come, O my God, the promise seal,
  This mountain sin remove;
  Now, in my waiting soul reveal
  The virtue of thy love.

2 I want thy life, thy purity,
  Thy righteousness brought in;
  I ask, desire, and trust in thee,
  To be redeemed from sin.

3 Saviour, to thee my soul looks up,
  My present Saviour thou!
  In all the confidence of hope,
  I claim the blessing now.

4 'Tis done: thou dost this moment save,
  With full salvation bless;
  Redemption through thy blood I have,
  And spotless love and peace.

61 Resting at the Cross.

W. J. K.

Music by WM. J. KIRKPATRICK.

1. To the cross of Christ, my Sav-iour, I had brought my wea-ry soul,
2. At the cross, while meekly bow-ing, Je - sus, smiling, bade me live;
3. At the cross, while prostrate ly - ing, Je - sus' blood flow'd o'er my soul;
4. At the cross I'm calm-ly rest-ing, Ev - 'ry moment now is sweet;

Burden'd, faint, and broken - hearted, Praying, "Je - sus, make me whole."
"I have died for your transgressions, And I free - ly all for - give."
All my guilt and sin were covered, And he whisper'd, "Child, be whole."
I am tast - ing of his glo - ry, I am rest-ing at his feet."

CHORUS.

Glo - ry, glo - ry be to Je - sus, I am counting all but dross,

I have found a full sal - va - tion, I am rest-ing at the cross;

I'm resting at the cross, I'm resting at the cross, I'm resting at the cross.

By permission.

56

62 Surrendered at Last.

DR. L. MASON.

1. Come, my fond flutt'ring heart,
Come, thou must now be free;
Thou and the world must part,
How-ev-er hard it be. My weeping passions own 'tis just, Yet cling still closer
to the dust. Yet cling.. still clos - - - - er to the... dust.
Yet cling, etc.

2 Ye tempting sweets, forbear,
  Ye dearest idols, fall;
My heart ye cannot share,
  For Jesus must have all.
'Tis bitter pain,—'tis cruel smart,
But O! you must consent, my heart.
3 Ye gay, enchanting throng,
  Ye golden dreams, farewell!
Earth hath prevail'd too long,

Now I must break the spell.
Go, cherish'd plans of earlier years,
Jesus, forgive these parting tears.
4 Welcome, O bleeding cross,
  Thou only way to God;
My former gains were loss,
  My path was folly's road.
At last my heart is undeceived,
The world is given, and Christ received.

63 REJOICE, THE LORD IS KING.

1 Rejoice, the Lord is King;
  Your Lord and King adore;
Mortals, give thanks and sing,
  And triumph evermore.
Lift up your hearts, lift up your voice;
Rejoice, again I say, rejoice.
2 Jesus, the Saviour, reigns,
  The God of truth and love;
When he had purged our stains,
  He took his seat above.
Lift up your hearts, lift up your voice;
Rejoice, again I say, rejoice.
3 His kingdom cannot fail —
  He rules o'er earth and heaven;
The keys of death and hell
  Are to our Jesus given.
Lift up your hearts, lift up your voice;
Rejoice, again I say, rejoice.

4 He sits at God's right hand
  Till all his foes submit,
And bow to his command,
  And fall beneath his feet.
Lift up your hearts, lift up your voice;
Rejoice, again I say, rejoice.
5 He all his foes shall quell,
  And all our sins destroy;
Let every bosom swell
  With pure seraphic joy.
Lift up your hearts, lift up your voice;
Rejoice, again I say, rejoice.
6 Rejoice in glorious hope;
  Jesus, the Judge, shall come
And take his servants up
  To their eternal home.
We soon shall hear th' archangel's voice;
(57) The trump of God shall sound,—Rejoice!

64   Full Salvation.

Words by CARRIE M. WILSON.   Music by JNO. R. SWENEY.

1. In the bright and shin-ing way   we   are marching on - ward still,
2. We are one in Christ, the Lord, and   a - bid - ing   in   his love,
3. We can read our ti - tle clear   to   a man - sion in   the sky,
4. We are trust-ing in   his grace, we   will trust him ev - er - more,

Liv-ing in   a full sal-va - tion; We are giv-ing up our all   to   the
Liv-ing in   a full sal-va - tion; We are look-ing for a home with the
Liv-ing in   a full sal-va - tion; We shall gath - er with the Lord in   his
Liv-ing in   a full sal-va - tion; O   the song that we shall sing when we

D.S. E - den here below, when such

Fine.

Blessed Master's will, And we praise him for a full   sal - va - tion.
hap - py ones a-bove, There to praise him for a full   sal - va - tion.
kingdom by and by, There to praise him for a full   sal - va - tion.
reach the oth-er shore, There to praise him for a full   sal - va - tion.

perfect peace we know. Hal-le - lu - jah! for   a full   sal - va - tion.

CHORUS.

Full   sal - va - tion, Hal - le - lu - jah to   his name!

D.S.

Full   sal - va-tion through his pre - cious blood we claim: What an

Revive Us.

Words by FANNY J. CROSBY.　　　　　　　　Music by JNO. R. SWENEY.

1. We come in our weakness, we come in our need; O, blessed Redeemer, thy
2. O give us more boldness to stand up for thee, And help us in labor more
3. O cleanse us a - new by thy Spirit within; We ask that this moment the

mer - its we plead, While here at thy al - tar we gather once more, Where
ear - nest to be; More watchful and prayerful, more gentle and meek, More
work may be - gin; We ask for more courage, when tempted and tried, More

CHORUS.

oft thou hast met and refresh'd us be-fore.　Revive us, revive us, dear
pa-tient in try - ing poor sin-ners to seek.
faith in the promise that thou wilt provide.

Saviour, we pray, And take from our hearts ev'ry idol a-way; Re - vive us, re -

vive us, now kindle a flame Of love in our souls that our tongues shall proclaim.

66   Is not this the Land of Beulah?

ANON.   ARRANGED.

1. I am dwell-ing on the mountain, Where the gold-en sunlight gleams
2. I can see far down the mountain, Where I wandered wea-ry years,
3. I am drink-ing at the fountain, Where I ev-er would a-bide;

O'er a land whose wondrous beauty   Far ex-ceeds my fond-est dreams;
Oft-en hindered in my journey   By the ghosts of doubts and fears,
For I've tast-ed life's pure riv-er,   And my soul is sat-is-fied;

Where the air is pure, e-the-real, La-den with the breath of flowers,
Bro-ken vows and dis-ap-point-ments Thickly sprinkled all the way,
There's no thirst-ing for life's pleasures, Nor a-dorn-ing, rich and gay,

Cho.-Is not this the land of Beu-lah? Blessed, bles-sed land of light,

D. S. Chorus.

They are blooming by the fountain, 'Neath the am-a-ran-thine bow'rs.
But the Spir-it led, un-err-ing, To the land I hold to-day.
For I've found a rich-er treasure, One that fad-eth not a-way.

Where the flow-ers bloom for-ev-er, And the sun is always bright.

4 Tell me not of heavy crosses,
  Nor the burdens hard to bear,
For I've found this great salvation
  Makes each burden light appear;
And I love to follow Jesus,
  Gladly counting all but dross,
Worldly honors all forsaking
  For the glory of the Cross.

5 Oh, the Cross has wondrous glory!
  Oft I've proved this to be true;
When I'm in the way so narrow,
  I can see a pathway through;
And how sweetly Jesus whispers:
  Take the Cross, thou need'st not fear,
For I've tried the way before thee,
  And the glory lingers near.

67   I'm Redeemed.

T. C. O'K.

Music by T. C. O'KANE.

1. O. sing of Je-sus, "Lamb of God," Who died on Cal - va - ry,
2. O wondrous pow'r of love di-vine! So pure, so full, so free!
3. All glo - ry now to Christ the Lord, And ev - er - more shall be:

And for a ran-som shed his blood, For you and e - ven me.
It reaches out to all mankind, Em-brac - es e - ven me.
He hath redeem'd a world from sin, And ransom'd e - ven me.

REFRAIN.

I'm re - deem'd,...... I'm re - deem'd,...... Through the

I'm re-deem'd,   I'm re-deem'd,

blood of the Lamb that was slain;...... I'm re - deem'd......

of the Lamb that was slain.   I'm redeem'd,

I'm re - deem'd,.... Hal - le - lu - jah un - to his name.

I'm re-deem'd,

Trusting in the Promise.

H. B. H.

Music by E. S. LORENZ. By per.

1. I have found repose for my weary soul, Trusting in the promise of the Saviour;
2. I will sing my song as the days go by, Trusting in the promise of the Saviour;
3. O, the peace and joy of the life I live, Trusting in the promise of the Saviour;

Fine.

And a harbor safe when the billows roll, Trusting in the promise of the Saviour.
And rejoice in hope, while I live or die, Trusting in the promise of the Saviour.
O, the strength and grace only God can give, Trusting in the promise of the Saviour.

D.S. I will rest by grace in his strong embrace, Trusting in the promise of the Saviour.

I will fear no foe in the deadly strife, Trusting in the promise of the Saviour;
I can smile at grief and abide in pain, Trusting in the promise of the Saviour;
Whosoever will may be sav'd to-day, Trusting in the promise of the Saviour;

I will bear my lot in the toil of life, Trusting in the promise of the Saviour.
And the loss of all shall be highest gain, Trusting in the promise of the Saviour.
And begin to walk in the ho-ly way, Trusting in the promise of the Saviour.

REFRAIN.

D.S.

Resting on his mighty arm for-ev - er, Never from his loving heart to sev-er.

From " HEAVENLY CAROLS," by per.

69   The Stranger at the Door.

Music by T. C. O'KANE. By per.

With feeling.

1. Be - hold a stranger at the door; He gently knocks—has knock'd before;
2. O love - ly at - ti - tude—he stands With melting heart and load - ed hands;
3. But will he prove a friend indeed? He will—the ver - y friend you need:
4. Rise, touch'd with gratitude divine; Turn out his en - e - my and thine:
5. Ad - mit him, ere his an-ger burn—His feet, de-part - ed, ne'er re-turn;

Has wait-ed long, is waiting still: You treat no oth - er friend so ill.
O matchless kindness—and he shows This matchless kindness to his foes.
The friend of sin-ners? Yes,'tis he, With garments dyed on Cal - va-ry.
That soul-destroying monster—sin, And let the Heav'nly Stranger in.
Ad - mit him, or the hour's at hand, You'll at *his* door re - ject - ed stand.

REFRAIN.

O, let the dear Saviour come in, He'll cleanse the heart from sin;
come in, from sin;

O, keep him no more out at the door, But let the dear Saviour come in.
come in.

70 Over the Threshold.

Words by FRANK GOULD.　　　　　　　　　　　Music by JNO. R. SWENEY.

1. Step o - ver the threshold, and wan-der no more, Oppress'd with the
2. Step o - ver the threshold, let faith be thy guide To him, thy Phy-
3. Step o - ver the threshold, re - pent and be - lieve, And quick-ly thy
4. Step o - ver the threshold, no ref - uge hast thou, No hope of re -

bur - den of sin;　Step o - ver the threshold, why stand at the door, The
si - cian so kind;　Go　wash in the fountain that flows from his side, And
bur - den will fall;　O　touch but his garments, and thou shalt receive The
demption but he:　Step o - ver the threshold, and come to him now, O

D S. o - ver the threshold, why stand at the door, Come

Fine. CHORUS.

Heal - er is wait - ing with-in.　　　Then come as thou art; thy
health to thy soul thou shalt find.
par - don he of - fers to all.
lost one, he tar - ries for thee.

in, there is mer - cy for thee.

D. S.

poor broken heart Re - new'd by his spir-it shall be;　Step

The Blessed Exchange.

Words by P. J. OWENS. Music by WM. J. KIRKPATRICK.

1. Have you pov - er - ty and sor-row? Christ has rich - es true:
2. Have you tri - als and temp-ta - tion? Christ has strength and grace:
3. Have you darkness, doubt and er - ror? Christ has light and truth:
4. Have you weakness? he has pow-er! Have you pain and strife?
5. Let his love, your heart pos - ses-sing, All your sins de - stroy;

Come to him and free - ly bor - row, He will give to you.
He will give a full sal - va - tion, If you seek his face.
Death and judgment bring you ter - ror? Christ has words to soothe.
Christ has help for ev - 'ry hour, Christ is peace and life.
He will change your wants to bless-ing, Change your grief to joy.

CHORUS.

Come and exchange, Come and exchange; Bring all your wants to Je - sus:

Lay your sins aside, In his faith and love abide, And you shall have wealth in Jesus.

72 Wilt thou be made whole?

W. J. K.   Music by Wm. J. Kirkpatrick.

1. Hear the footsteps of Je - sus, He is now passing by, Bearing balm for the
2. 'Tis the voice of that Saviour Whose mer-ci - ful call Free-ly of-fers sal-
3. Are you halting and struggling, O'erpow'rd by your sin, While the waters are
4. Bless-ed Saviour, as - sist us To rest on thy word; Let the soul healing

wounded, Healing all who ap-ply; As he spake to the suff'rer Who
va - tion To one and to all; He is now beck'ning to him Each
troubled, Can you not en - ter in? Lo, the Saviour stands waiting To
pow - er On us now be outpour'd: Wash a - way ev - 'ry sin-spot, Take

lay at the pool, He is say-ing this moment, "Wilt thou be made whole?"
sin - taint-ed soul, And lov-ing-ly asking, "Wilt thou be made whole?"
strengthen your soul, He is earnest-ly pleading, "Wilt thou be made whole?"
per - fect con-trol, Say to each trusting spirit, "Thy faith makes thee whole."

REFRAIN.

Wilt thou be made whole? Wilt thou be made whole? O come, wea-ry

suff'rer, O come, sin-sick soul; See, the life-stream is flowing, See, the

Wilt thou be made whole? Concluded.

cleansing waves roll: Step in - to the cur-rent and thou shalt be whole.

73 Satisfied.

Words by Miss CLARA TEARE. Music by R. E. HUDSON.

1. All my life long I had pant-ed For a draught from some cool spring,
2. Feeding on the husks a-round me, Till my strength was al-most gone,
3. Poor I was, and sought for rich-es, Something that would sat - is - fy,
4. Well of wa - ter, ev - er springing, Bread of life, so rich and free,

That I hop'd would quench the burning Of the thirst I felt with-in.
Long'd my soul for something bet-ter, On - ly still to hun-ger on.
But the dust I gathered round me On - ly mock'd my soul's sad cry.
Un - told wealth that nev-er fail-eth, My Re - deem-er is to me.

CHORUS.

Hal-le - lu - jah! I have found him—Whom my soul so long has crav'd!

Je-sus sat - is - fies my longings; Thro' his blood I now am sav'd.

From "GEMS OF GOSPEL SONGS," by per.

67

The Prodigal Son.

Arr. by H. C. WATSON.

Solemnly, with feeling.

1. Af - flictions, tho' they seem se-vere, In mer - cy oft are sent;
2. What have I gain'd by sin, he said, But hun-ger, shame, and fear:
3. I'll go and tell him all I've done, Fall down be-fore his face,
4. His Fa - ther saw him com-ing back, He saw, he ran, he smil'd,
5. O Fa - ther, I have sinn'd, forgive—E-nough, the Fa - ther said:

Fine.

They stopp'd the prod-i - gal's ca-reer, And caus'd him to re - pent.
My Fa-ther's house abounds in bread, While I am starving here.
Un - wor-thy to be call'd his son, I'll seek a servant's place.
And threw his arms a - round the neck Of his re - bellious child!
Re - joice, my house, my son's a - live, For whom I mourn'd as dead!

D.S. My Fa-ther's house hath large supplies, And bounteous are his hands.

CHORUS.

I'll not die here for bread, I'll not die here for bread, he cries, Nor

Chorus for fourth, fifth, sixth and seventh verses.

I'll die no more for bread, I'll die no more for bread, he cries, Nor

D.S.

starve in for - eign lands:

6 Now let the fatted calf be slain,
And spread the news around:
My son was dead, and lives again,
Was lost, but now is found.
I'll die no more, &c.

7 'Tis thus the Lord his love reveals,
To call poor sinners home:
More than a father's love he feels,
And welcomes all that come.
I'll die no more, &c.

75 The Half has Never been Told.

Words by FRANCES RIDLEY HAVERGAL.   Music by R. E. HUDSON. By p r.

1. I know I love thee bet-ter, Lord, Than an - y earth - ly joy;
2. I know that thou art near-er still Than an - y earth - ly throng,
3. Thou hast put glad-ness in my heart; Then may I well be glad!
4. O, Sav-iour, precious Saviour, mine! What will thy presence be

For thou hast giv-en me the peace Which noth-ing can de - stroy.
And sweet-er is the thought of thee Than an - y love - ly song.
Without the se-cret of thy love I could not but be sad.
If such a life of joy can crown Our walk on earth with thee?

CHORUS.

The half has never yet been told,   Of love so full and free;
                    yet been told,

The half has never yet been told,   The blood—it cleanseth me.
                    yet been told,   cleanseth me.

rit.

From "GEMS OF GOSPEL SONGS."

69

Sweetly Resting.

(Dedicated to Chaplain C. C. McCabe.)

Words by MARY D. JAMES.　　　　Music by W. WARREN BENTLEY. By per.

1. In the rift-ed Rock I'm rest-ing, Safe-ly shelter'd I a-bide;
2. Long pur-sued by sin and Sa-tan, Weary, sad, I long'd for rest;
3. Peace, which passeth un-der-stand-ing, Joy, the world can nev-er give,
4. In the rift-ed Rock I'll hide me, Till the storms of life are past,

There no foes nor storms molest me, While within the cleft I hide.

Then I found this heav'nly shelter, Opened in my Saviour's breast.

Now in Je-sus I am finding: In his smiles of love I live.

All se-cure in this blest refuge, Heeding not the fiercest blast.

REFRAIN.

Now I'm resting, Sweetly resting, In the cleft once made for me:

Je-sus, blessed Rock of A-ges, I will hide my-self in thee.

77   I rest upon His Promise.

Words by CHARLES WESLEY.   Music by R. E. HUDSON.

1. Lord, I be-lieve a rest re-mains To all thy peo - ple known;
2. A rest, where all our soul's de - sire Is fix'd on things a - bove;
3. Oh! that I now the rest might know, Be - lieve, and en - ter in;
4. Re - move this hardness from my heart, This un - be - lief, re - move;

A rest where pure en-joy-ment reigns, And thou art lov'd a - lone.
Where fear, and sin, and grief ex - pire, Cast out by per - fect love.
Now, Sav-iour, now the pow'r be - stow, And let me cease from sin.
To me the rest of faith im - part—The Sab-bath of thy love.

CHORUS.

I rest up - on his promise, sure; I come, I wait to prove

The cleansing of my heart from sin, The full - ness of his love.

From "GEMS OF GOSPEL SONGS," by per.

78 Rock in the Desert.

Words by FANNY J. CROSBY.　　　　　　　　　　　　　　Music by JNO. R. SWENEY.

1. Rock in the desert, my shield from the blast, Un-der thy shadow I'm
2. Rock in the desert, how love-ly the star Guiding my footsteps from
3. Rock in the desert, how peaceful my rest, Kindly pro-tect-ed, no
4. Rock in the desert, O Sav-iour di-vine, Thou art my refuge, no

hid - ing at last; Dear is thy refuge, and welcome to me; Rock in the
wand'ring a - far; Now I am happy, thy shel-ter I see; Rock in the
long - er oppress'd; Long have I thirsted for streams cool and free, Rock in the
love is like thine; Thou my Re-deem-er art gracious to me: Rock in the

My soul flies to thee, My

CHORUS.

desert, my soul flies to thee. My soul flies to thee, My soul flies to thee, My
desert, my faith clings to thee.
desert, I find them in thee.
desert, I live but in thee.

soul flies to thee.

soul flies to thee, My soul flies to thee. Rock in the desert,

Rock in the desert, Rock in the desert, my soul flies to thee.

79 The Angels are Looking on Me!

Rev. John Parker. — Arranged for this Work.

1. Like Ja-cob, in his Bethel rest, The an - gels are looking on me;
2. Each night I lay me down to sleep, The an - gels are looking on me;
3. And when I wake, new toils to meet, The an - gels are looking on me;
4. A pil - grim to the heav'nly land, The an - gels are looking on me;
5. And till I reach my home at last, The an - gels are looking on me;

They watch my pil-low—I am blest, The an - gels are looking on me.
I know I'm safe, for an - gels keep, The an - gels are looking on me.
God's presence makes my joy complete, The an - gels are looking on me.
My steps are kept by God's command, The an - gels are looking on me.
With ev - 'ry tear and tri - al past, The an - gels are looking on me.

REFRAIN.

All night, all night, the an - gels are look-ing on me;

All night, all night, The an - gels are look-ing on me!

80   Pentecostal Power.

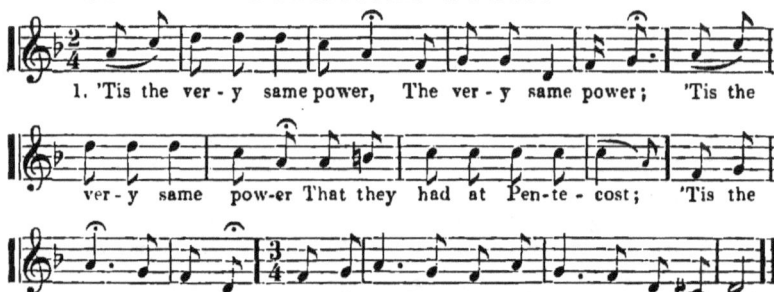

1. 'Tis the ver - y same power, The ver - y same power; 'Tis the
ver - y same pow-er That they had at Pen - te - cost; 'Tis the
pow'r, the pow-er; 'Tis the pow'r that Je-sus promis'd should come down.

2 While with one accord assembled,
  All in an upper room,
    Came the power, etc.

3 With cloven tongues of fire,
  And a rushing mighty wind,
    Came the power, etc.

4 'Twas while they were all praying,
  And believing it would come,
    Came the power, etc.

5 Some thought they were fanatic,
  Or were drunken with new wine:
    'Twas the power, etc.

6 Three thousand were converted,
  And were added to the church,
    By the power, etc.

7 The martyrs had this power,
  As they triumphed in the flames;
    'Twas the power, etc.

8 Our fathers had this power,
  And we may have it too;
    'Tis the power, etc.

9 'Tis the very same power,
  For I feel it in my soul;
    'Tis the power, etc.

---

81   Northfield.   C. M.

1 I know that my Redeemer lives,
  And ever prays for me;
  A token of his love he gives —
    A pledge of liberty.

2 I find him lifting up my head:
  He brings salvation near;
  His presence makes me free indeed,
    And he will soon appear.

3 He wills that I should holy be!
  What can withstand his will?

The counsel of his grace in me
  He surely shall fulfil.

4 Jesus, I hang upon thy word;
  I steadfastly believe
  Thou wilt return and claim me, Lord,
    And to thyself receive.

5 When God is mine, and I am his,
  Of paradise possess'd,
  I taste unutterable bliss
    And everlasting rest.

---

82   JESUS, UNITED BY THY GRACE.

1 Jesus, united by thy grace,
  And each to each endear'd,
  With confidence we seek thy face,
  And know our prayer is heard.

2 Still let us own our common Lord,
  And bear thine easy yoke —
  A band of love, a threefold chord,
  Which never can be broke.

3 Make us into one spirit drink;
  Baptize into thy name;

And let us always kindly think
  And sweetly speak the same.

4 Touch'd by the loadstone of thy love,
  Let all our hearts agree;
  And ever toward each other move,
  And ever move toward thee.

5 To thee, inseparably join'd,
  Let all our spirits cleave;
  O may we all the loving mind
  That was in thee receive.

(74)

Glorious Fountain.

W. COWPER.

T. C. O'KANE.

1. { There is a fountain fill'd with blood, fill'd with blood, fill'd with blood,
   { And sinners plung'd beneath that flood, beneath that flood, beneath that flood,
2. { The dy-ing thief re-joic'd to see, re-joic'd to see, re-joic'd to see,
   { And there may I, though vile as he, tho' vile as he, tho' vile as he,

There is a fountain, fill'd with blood, Drawn from Immanuel's veins, }
And sinners plung'd beneath that flood, Lose all their guilty stains. }
The dy-ing thief re-joic'd to see That fountain in his day, }
And there may I, though vile as he, Wash all my sins a - way. }

CHORUS.

Oh, glo-ri-ous fountain! Here will I stay, And in thee ev - er

Wash my sins a - way.

3
Thou dying Lamb, ‖: thy precious blood :‖
Shall never lose its power,
Till all the ransomed ‖: Church of God :‖
Are saved, to sin no more.

4
E'er since by faith ‖: I saw the stream :‖
Thy flowing wounds supply,
Redeeming love ‖: has been my theme, :‖
And shall be till I die.

From "REDEEMER'S PRAISE," by per.

84
I Need Thee.

Words by FRANK GOULD.　　　　　　　　　　　　Music by JNO. R. SWENEY.

1. Blessed Sav - iour, my Re-deem-er, In thy mer - cy, hear my call;
2. Yes, I need thee, blessed Saviour, I am weak and poor in - deed;
3. How I need thee, when the sunshine Of a calm de-light I share;

How I need thy grace to keep me, Every mo - ment, lest I fall.
And I need the bread thou givest, Bread of life, my soul to feed.
How I need thee, when my burden Is too great for me to bear.

Lord, I need thy hand to guide me Wheresoe'er my path may be;
Still I need thy strength to arm me 'Gainst the man - y foes with-in;
Lord, in life and death I need thee, For I live but in thy smile;

O! I need thy love so ten-der, None can ev - er love like thee.
Still I need thy blood to cleanse me, And to keep my heart from sin.
O! I need thee, blessed Sav-iour, Yes, I need thee all the while.

CHORUS.

Bend thou thine ear, Thy promise all my plea ; I need thy love, thy tender love,

I Need Thee. Concluded.

O! grant it, Lord, to me, O! grant it, Lord, to me.
now to me, now to me.

85

Jesus Saves Me.

Words by MANIE PAYNE. Music by WM. J. KIRKPATRICK. By per.

1. Je - sus saves me, this I know, Un-der-neath the crimson flow;
2. Sin-ful though my na - ture be, Je - sus died to set me free;
3. Failures, Je - sus nev - er knew; What he promis'd he can do;
4. In the twinkling of an eye, Je - sus' blood can sanc-ti - fy;

He has wash'd a - way my sin, Made me white and pure with-in.
Died that sin might be destroy'd, Died, that love might fill the void.
And the al - tar sanc-ti - fies Me, a liv - ing sac - ri - fice.
Trust-ing - ly my all I give, Per - fect cleansing I re - ceive.

CHORUS.

Yes, Jesus saves me, Yes, Jesus saves me, Yes, Jesus saves me, And cleanses me from sin.

86 Waiting for Me.

Words by FRANK HENDRICKS.　　　　　　　　　Music by JNO. R. SWENEY.

1. I came to the fountain that cleanseth from sin, The life-giving
2. He saw me approaching, and ten-der-ly said—To purchase thy
3. I flew to his mer-cy, O joy-ful sur-prise, For lo, my Re-
4. And now in his presence I walk with de-light, And feel his pro-

fountain where millions have been; I came in my weak-ness, o'er
ran-som, my blood I have shed; And if thou art willing just
deem-er had opened mine eyes; I flew to the refuge no
tect-ion by day and by night; I think of the fountain so

burdened with care, To find my Re-deem-er and Saviour was there.
now to be-lieve, The light of my Spir-it thy soul shall re-ceive.
oth-er could give, And faith-ful-ly promised for Je-sus to live.
precious and free, Where Jesus, my Saviour, was waiting for me.

Wait - - - ing for me,...... wait - - - ing for me,......

CHORUS.

Waiting for me, waiting for me, waiting for me, waiting for me,

Je - - - sus, my Sav - iour, is wait - - - ing for me;......

Jesus, my Saviour, is waiting for me, Jesus, my Saviour, is waiting for me;

Waiting for Me. Concluded.

Still...... at the Fount,.... oft........ would I be ...... Where

Still at the Fount, oft would I be, Still at the Fount, Oft would I be, Where

Je - - - - sus, my Sav - - iour, is wait - - ing for me.

Jesus, my Sav-iour, is waiting for me, is waiting, is waiting for me.

87   Hallelujah! Amen.

HENRIETTA E. BLAIR.   Adapted and arr. by WM. J. KIRKPATRICK.

1. How oft in holy converse With Christ, my Lord, alone, I seem to hear the
2. They pass'd thro' toils and trials, And tho' the strife was long, They share the victor's
3. My soul takes up the cho-rus, And pressing on my way, Communing still with
4. Thro' grace I soon shall conquer, And reach my home on high; And thro' eternal

CHORUS.

millions That sing around his throne:— Hal-le - lu-jah, A-men. Hal-le -
conquest, And sing the victor's song.
Je - sus, I sing from day to day.
a - ges I'll shout beyond the sky.

poco rit.

lu - jah, A - men. Hal - le - lu - jah, A - men. A - men, A - men.

Copyright, 1885, *by W. J. KIRKPATRICK.*

88 Blessed Assurance.

Words by FANNIE CROSBY.   Music by Mrs. JOS. F. KNAPP. By per.

1. Blessed as - sur-ance, Je - sus is mine! Oh, what a fore - taste of
2. Perfect sub-mis-sion, per - fect de-light, Visions of rap - ture burst
3. Perfect sub-mis-sion, all is at rest, I in my Sav - iour am

glo - ry di-vine! Heir of sal-va-tion, purchased of God, Born of his
on my sight; An - gels descending, bring from a - bove Echoes of
hap - py and blest; Watching and waiting, looking a - bove, Fill'd with his

CHORUS.

Spir - it, wash'd in his blood. This is my sto - ry, this is my
mer - cy, whispers of love.
goodness, lost in his love.

song, Praising my Sav-iour all the day long; This is my sto - ry,

this is my song, Praising my Saviour all the day long.

1 Bless'd be the tie that binds
  Our hearts in Christian love;
The fellowship of kindred minds
  Is like to that above.

2 Before our Father's throne,
  We pour our ardent prayers;
Our fears, our hopes, our aims are one,
  Our comforts and our cares.

3 We share our mutual woes;
  Our mutual burdens bear;
And often for each other flows
  The sympathizing tear.

4 When we asunder part,
  It gives us inward pain;
But we shall still be join'd in heart,
  And hope to meet again.

5 This glorious hope revives
  Our courage by the way;
While each in expectation lives,
  And longs to see the day.

6 From sorrow, toil and pain,
  And sin, we shall be free;
And perfect love and friendship reign
  Through all eternity.   J. FAWCETT.

---

90   OH, NOW I SEE THE CRIMSON WAVE.   (B. S. 5.)

1 Oh, now I see the crimson wave,
  The fountain deep and wide;
Jesus, my Lord, mighty to save,
  Points to his wounded side.
    Chorus.
The cleansing stream I see, I see!
I plunge, and oh, it cleanseth me!
Oh, praise the Lord, it cleanseth me!
It cleanseth me, yes, cleanseth me!

2 I see the new creation rise;
  I hear the speaking blood!

It speaks! polluted nature dies!
  Sinks 'neath the cleansing flood.

3 I rise to walk in heaven's own light,
  Above the world and sin;   [white,
With heart made pure, and garments
  And Christ enthroned within.

4 Amazing grace! 'tis heaven below,
  To feel the blood applied,
And Jesus, only Jesus know,
  My Jesus crucified.
                PHOEBE PALMER.

---

91   HE LEADETH ME!

1 He leadeth me! oh! blessed thought,
Oh! words with heavenly comfort fraught
Whate'er I do, where'er I be,
Still 'tis God's hand that leadeth me!
    Refrain.
He leadeth me! he leadeth me!
By his own hand he leadeth me;
His faithful follower I would be,
For by his hand he leadeth me.

2 Sometimes 'mid scenes of deepest gloom,
Sometimes where Eden's bowers bloom,

By waters still, o'er troubled sea —
Still 'tis his hand that leadeth me.

3 Lord, I would clasp thy hand in mine,
Nor ever murmur, nor repine—
Content, whatever lot I see,
Since 'tis my God that leadeth me.

4 And when my task on earth is done,
When, by thy grace, the victory's won,
E'en death's cold wave I will not flee,
Since God through Jordan leadeth me.
            Rev Jos. H. GILMORE.

---

92   THE GREAT PHYSICIAN NOW IS NEAR.   (B. S. 35.)

1 The great Physician now is near,
  The sympathizing Jesus:
He speaks the drooping heart to cheer,
  Oh, hear the voice of Jesus.
    Chorus.
Sweetest note in seraph song,
Sweetest name on mortal tongue;
Sweetest carol ever sung,—
Jesus, Jesus, Jesus.

2 Your many sins are all forgiven,
  Oh! hear the voice of Jesus:
Go on your way in peace to heav'n,
  And wear a crown with Jesus.

3 All glory to the dying Lamb,
  I now believe in Jesus:
I love the blessed Saviour's name,
  I love the name of Jesus.

4 His name dispels my guilt and fear,
  No other name but Jesus:
Oh! how my soul delights to hear
  The charming name of Jesus.

5 And when to that bright world above
  We rise to see our Jesus,
We'll sing around the throne of love,
  The name, the name of Jesus.

93 Nothing but the Blood of Jesus.

R. L.

Music by R. LOWRY. By per.

1. { What can wash a - way my sin? Nothing but the blood of Je - sus. }
     { What can make me whole a - gain? Nothing but the blood of Je - sus. }

CHORUS.

Oh, precious is the flow That makes me white as snow:

No oth - er Fount I know, Nothing but the blood of Je - sus.

2 For my pardon this I see —
Nothing but the blood of Jesus;
For my cleansing, this my plea, —
Nothing but the blood of Jesus. — *Cho.*

3 Nothing can for sin atone,
Nothing but the blood of Jesus;

Naught of good that I have done,
Nothing but the blood of Jesus. — *Cho.*

4 This is all my hope and peace —
Nothing but the blood of Jesus;
This is all my righteousness —
Nothing but the blood of Jesus. — *Cho.*

94 Glory to the Lamb.

Rev. B. W. GORHAM.

1. The world is overcome by the blood of the Lamb. Glory to the Lamb, Glory

to the Lamb, Glory to the Lamb.

2 My sins are wash'd away,
In the blood of the Lamb.

3 I've wash'd my garments white,
In the blood of the Lamb.

4 The martyrs overcame,
By the blood of the Lamb.

5 I soon shall gain the skies,
Through the blood of the Lamb.

95 Jesus will give you Rest.

Words by FANNY J. CROSBY.　　　　　　　Music by JNO. R. SWENEY. By per.

1. Will you come, will you come, with your poor broken heart, Burden'd and sin op-
2. Will you come, will you come? there is mer-cy for you, Balm for your ach-ing
3. Will you come, will you come, you have nothing to pay; Je-sus, who loves you
4. Will you come, will you come? how he pleads with you now! Fly to his lov-ing

press'd?　Lay it down　at the feet　of your Sav - iour and Lord,
breast;　On - ly come　as you are,　and be - lieve　on his name,
best,　By his death　on the Cross　purchas'd life　for your soul,
breast,　And what-ev - er your sin　or your sor - row may be,

REFRAIN.

Je - sus will give　you　rest.　Oh, happy rest, sweet, happy rest!

Je - sus will give　you　rest.　Oh! why won't you come in

happy rest,

sim - ple, trust - ing faith? Je - sus will give　you　rest.

From "JOY TO THE WORLD."

96 Happy Tidings.

Words by LIZZIE EDWARDS. Music by JNO. R. SWENEY. By per.

1. Tidings, happy tidings, Hark! hark! the sound! Hear the joy-ful ech-o
2. Tidings, happy tidings, Hark! hark! they say, Do not slight the warning,
3. Tidings, happy tidings, Hark! hark! a-gain! Rushing o'er the mountain,

Thro' the world resound; Christ the Lord proclaims them, Hear and heed the call:
Come, O come to-day. Christ, our lov-ing Saviour, Still repeats the call—
Sweep-ing o'er the plain; On-ward goes the message, 'Tis the Saviour's call:

REFRAIN.

Come ye starving ones that perish, Room, room for all. Who-so-ev-er ask-eth,
Come ye wea-ry, hea-vy la-den, Room, room for all.
Come, for ev-'ry thing is ready, Room, room for all.

Jesus will receive; Whosoever thirsteth, Jesus will relieve. See the liv-ing

waters, Flowing full and free; O the blessed who-so-ev-er, That means me.

From "SONGS OF TRIUMPH."

84

97 Jesus, I my Cross have taken. 8, 7. D.

Words by HENRY F. LYTE.

Arr. from JOHANN C. W. A. MOZART.

1. Je-sus, I my cross have taken, All to leave and fol-low thee;

Naked, poor, despised, for-sa-ken, Thou from hence my all shalt be:

D. S.—Yet how rich is my con-di-tion, God and heav'n are still my own.

Per-ish ev-'ry fond am-bi-tion, All I've sought, and hop'd, and known;

2 Let the world despise and leave me,
　They have left my Saviour too;
Human hearts and looks deceive me;
　Thou art not, like man, untrue:
And, while thou shalt smile upon me,
　God of wisdom, love and might,
Foes may hate, and friends may shun me;
　Show thy face, and all is bright.

3 Go, then, earthly fame and treasure!
　Come, disaster, scorn and pain!
In thy service, pain is pleasure;
　With thy favor, loss is gain.
I have called thee, "Abba, Father;"
　I have stayed my heart on thee:
Storms may howl, and clouds may gather,
　All must work for good to me.

4 Man may trouble and distress me,
　'Twill but drive me to thy breast;
Life with trials hard may press me,
　Heaven will bring me sweeter rest.

O 'tis not in grief to harm me,
　While thy love is left to me;
O 'twere not in joy to charm me,
　Were that joy unmixed with thee.

5 Know, my soul, thy full salvation;
　Rise o'er sin, and fear, and care;
Joy to find in every station
　Something still to do or bear.
Think what Spirit dwells within thee;
　What a Father's smile is thine;
What a Saviour died to win thee:
　Child of heaven, shouldst thou repine?

6 Haste thee on from grace to glory,
　Armed by faith, and winged by prayer;
Heaven's eternal day's before thee,
　God's own hand shall guide thee there.
Soon shall close thy earthly mission,
　Swift shall pass thy pilgrim days,
Hope shall change to glad fruition,
　Faith to sight, and prayer to praise.

85

98   Yield not to Temptation.

Words and Music by H. R. PALMER.

1. Yield not to temptation, For yielding is sin; Each vict'ry will help you
2. Shun e - vil companions; Bad language disdain; God's name hold in rev'rence,
3. To him that o'ercometh God giveth a crown; Thro' faith we will conquer,

Some oth-er to win.   Fight manfully onward, Dark passions sub-due,
Nor take it in vain.   Be thoughtful and earnest, Kind-hearted and true,
Though often cast down.   He who is our Saviour, Our strength will re-new:

CHORUS.

Look ev-er to Je-sus, He'll carry you through. Ask the Saviour to help you,

Comfort, strengthen, and keep you, He is willing to aid you, He will carry you thro'.

By permission.

---

99   STAND UP FOR JESUS!

1 Stand up! stand up for Jesus!
  Ye soldiers of the cross;
Lift high his royal banner,
  It must not suffer loss:
From victory unto victory
  His army he shall lead,
Till every foe is vanquished,
  And Christ is Lord indeed.

2 Stand up! stand up for Jesus!
  Stand in his strength alone;
The arm of flesh will fail you,—
  Ye dare not trust your own:

Put on the gospel armor,
  And, watching unto prayer,
Where duty calls, or danger,
  Be never wanting there.

3 Stand up! stand up for Jesus!
  The strife will not be long;
This day the noise of battle,
  The next the victor's song:
To him that overcometh
  A crown of life shall be;
He with the King of Glory
  Shall reign eternally.

100 Enough for Me.

Words and Music by Rev. E. A. HOFFMAN. By per.

1. O love surpassing knowledge! O grace so full and free! I know that Jesus saves me,

know that Jesus saves me,

Fine. REFRAIN. D.S.

And that's enough for me! And that's enough for me! And that's enough for me! I

And that's enough for me!

2 O wonderful salvation!
From sin he makes me free!
I feel the sweet assurance,
And that's enough for me!

3 O blood of Christ so precious,
Poured out on Calvary!
I feel its cleansing power,
And that's enough for me!

---

101 OH, WONDROUS LOVE OF JESUS.

1 Oh, wondrous love of Jesus,
He tasted death for me;
He lives my King forever,
And that's enough for me.

2 His blessed Holy Spirit
With mine doth now agree;
He tells me—I'm adopted:
And that's enough for me.

3 I have his sweet communion,
He walks—and talks with me,

And fills my life with gladness—
And that's enough for me.

4 Oh uttermost Salvation,
A fountain full and free;
Its streams to all are flowing—
And that's enough for me.

5 His grace will be sufficient,
Till I his glory see;
Then safe at home forever—
And that's enough for me.

Rev. JOHN PARKER.

---

102 GOD LOVED THE WORLD OF SINNERS LOST. (B. S. 34.)

1 God loved the world of sinners lost
And ruined by the fall;
Salvation full, at highest cost,
He offers free to all.

Chorus.

O, 'twas love, 'twas wondrous love!
The love of God to me;
It brought my Saviour from above,
To die on Calvary.

2 E'en now by faith I claim him mine,
The risen Son of God;
Redemption by his death I find,
And cleansing through his blood.

3 Love brings the glorious fullness in,
And to his saints makes known,
The blessed rest from inbred sin,
Through faith in Christ alone.

4 Believing souls, rejoicing go;
There shall to you be given
A glorious foretaste here, below,
Of endless life in heaven.

5 Of victory now o'er Satan's power,
Let all the ransom'd sing;
And triumph in the dying hour,
Thro' Christ, the Lord, our King.

Mrs. M. STOCKTON.

103   Triumph! Triumph!

[Lines written on the last words of Rev. J. S. INSKIP.]

Dr. H. L. Gilmour.   Wm. J. Kirkpatrick. By per.

1. The gleaming spires of Beu - lah land   I trace with fail-ing sight;
2. My ransom'd spir - it plum'd for flight, The glo-rious con-flict o'er,
3. Sweet sounds from Beulah greet my ear,   I rev - el in the theme;
4. Farewell, dear friends, mourn not my loss, Sal-va - tion still pro-claim,

Its heav'nly land-scape fast ap-pears, As dark-ness ends in light.
O Death, where is thy vic-to-ry, I tri - umph as I soar.
Their "songs of tri-umph" I shall join, To him who did re-deem.
That all the sons of Adam's race May "triumph" thro' the Lamb.

CHORUS.

I "triumph" with a conqu'ring faith, Since Je - sus has cross'd o'er;

I "triumph" in my up-ward flight, I'll tri-umph ev - er-more.

104 Lo, the Golden Fields are Smiling.

Words by FANNY J. CROSBY.   Music by W. J. KIRKPATRICK. By per.

1. Lo, the golden fields are smil - ing, Where-fore idle shouldst thou be?
2. Take the balm of con-so-la - tion, That so oft has cheer'd thy heart;
3. Go and gather souls for Je - sus; Precious souls thy love may win;
4. Go, then work, the Master call - eth; Go, no longer i - dle be:

Great the harvest, few the work-ers, And the Lord hath need of thee.
Let some weary brother toil - er, In thy comfort share a part.
Lead them to the door of mer - cy, Tell them how to en - ter in.
Waste no more thy precious moments, For the Lord hath need of thee.

Go and work, the time is wan - ing, Let thy earnest heart re-ply
Go and lift the heavy bur - den He has struggled long to bear;
Go and gather souls for Je - sus; Work while strength and breath remain :
Once he gave his life thy ran - som, That thy soul with him might live.

ad lib.   *Fine.*

To the call so oft re-peat - ed,—"Bless-ed Master, here am I."
Go, and kneeling down beside him, Blend thy faith with his in prayer.
What are years of constant la - bor To the joy thou yet shalt gain?
Now the service he de-mand - eth, Can thy heart refuse to give?

D. S. Go and fill thy place a-mong them, For the Lord hath need of thee.

REFRAIN.   *D.S.*

Hark! the song, the song of busy workers, In the fields so fair to see;

The New Song.

Words by FLORA L. BEST. Music by JNO. R. SWENEY. By per.

Moderato.

1. There are songs of joy that I lov'd to sing, When my heart was blithe as a
2. There are strains of home that are dear as life, And I list to them oft 'mid the
3. Can my lips be mute, or my heart be sad, When the gra-cious Mas-ter hath
4. I shall catch the gleam of its jasper wall When I come to the gloom of the

bird in Spring; But the song I have learn'd is so full of cheer, That the
din of strife; But I know of a home that is wondrous fair, And I
made me glad? When he points where the many man-sions be, And
e-ven-fall, For I know that the shadows, dreary and dim, Have a

REFRAIN. Vivace.

dawn shines out in the darkness drear. O, the new, new song! O, the
sing the psalm they are singing there.
sweetly says "There is one for thee?"
path of light that will lead to him.

O, the new, new song!

new, new song! I can sing it now With the

O, the new, new song! I can sing just now

From "GEMS OF PRAISE."

The New Song. Concluded.

ran - - som'd throng: Pow-er and do-min-ion to him that shall
ransom'd, the ransom'd throng:

reign; that shall reign; Glo-ry and praise to the Lamb that was slain.

106 Whosoever.

Words by JAMES NICHOLSON. Music by JNO. R. SWENEY. By per.

1. I praise the Lord that one like me, For mer-cy may to Jesus flee:
2. I was to sin a wretched slave, But Je-sus died my soul to save:
3. I look by faith and see this word Stamp'd with the blood of Christ, my Lord:
4. I now be-lieve he saves my soul; His precious blood hath made me whole:

He says that who-so - ev - er will, May seek and find sal-va-tion still.

REFRAIN.

My Saviour's promise fail-eth never; He counts me in the Who-so-ev-er.

From "GEMS OF PRAISE."

107 Glory to God, Hallelujah!

Words by FANNY J. CROSBY.　　　　　　　　Music by W. J. KIRKPATRICK.

1. We are nev - er, nev - er wea - ry of the grand old song;
2. We are lost a - mid the rap-ture of re - deem - ing love;
3. We are go - ing to a pal - ace that is built of gold;
4. There we'll shout re-deem-ing mer - cy in a glad, new song;

Glo - ry to God, hal - le - lu - jah! We can sing it loud as
Glo - ry to God, hal - le - lu - jah! We are ris - ing on its
Glo - ry to God, hal - le - lu - jah! Where the King in all his
Glo - ry to God, hal - le - lu - jah! There we'll sing the praise of

ev - er, with our faith more strong: Glo - ry to God, hal - le - lu - jah!
pin-ions to the hills a - bove: Glo-ry to God, hal - le - lu - jah!
splendor we shall soon be - hold: Glo-ry to God, hal - le - lu - jah!
Je-sus with the blood-wash'd throng: Glo-ry to God, hal - le - lu - jah!

CHORUS.

O, the children of the Lord have a right to shout and sing, For the

way is growing bright and our souls are on the wing; We are going by and by to the pal-ace of a King! Glo-ry to God, hal-le-lu-jah!

108 He Came to Save Me.

Words by HENRIETTA E. BLAIR.   Music by WM. J. KIRKPATRICK.

1. When Je - sus laid his crown a-side, He came to save me; When on the cross he
2. In my poor heart he deigns to dwell, He came to save me; O, praise his name, I
3. With gen-tle hand he leads me still, He came to save me; And trusting him I
4. To him my faith with rapture clings, He came to save me; To him my heart looks

CHORUS.

bled and died, He came to save me. I'm so glad, I'm so glad,
know it well, He came to save me.
fear no ill, He came to save me. I'm so glad, I'm so glad,
up and sings, He came to save me.

1.

I'm so glad that Je - sus came, And grace is free,

2.

I'm so glad that Je - sus came, He (Omit........ came to save me.

109   Trusting Thee.

Words by FANNY J. CROSBY.   Music by JNO. R. SWENEY.

1. Thou to whom my life   I owe, Thou from whom my bless-ings flow;
2. Trusting thee in good   or ill, On thy promise lean - ing still,
3. 'Tis thine eye that nev - er sleeps, O'er my path a vig - il keeps;
4. Trusting thee for all   I need; Trusting, though my heart may bleed:

Rock E - ter - nal, hope di - vine, Light, whose beams for-ev - er shine.
There my rest, and on - ly there, Safe be-neath thy ten - der care.
'Tis thy voice that calms my fears, Thy dear hand that dries my tears.
Trusting till my soul shall rise To its home be - yond the skies.

CHORUS.

This a-lone my joy shall be: Loving, praising, trust-ing thee;

Trust-ing thee,   trust - ing thee, Lov-ing, praising, trust - ing thee.

Trust - ing thee, yes, trust - ing thee,

110 His Blood has made me Whole.

Words by FANNY J. CROSBY.   Music by WM. J. KIRKPATRICK.

1. I sought in tears my Saviour's cross, He turn'd and look'd on me:
2. With trembling step, be-neath its flood I plung'd my guilty soul,
3. O, love di - vine, where shall my tongue Its song of praise be - gin?
4. It gave me life, it gave me joy! With per - fect heal-ing pow'r

"Be-hold," he said, "the crimson fount Where flows my blood for thee!"
That now re-deem'd, can shout a - loud—His blood has made me whole!
The precious blood of Christ, my Lord, Has cov - er'd all my sin.
It sav'd through faith my broken heart, And saves me ev - 'ry hour.

CHORUS.

O, precious blood! oh, hallow'd blood! Thy sa - cred fount I see:

It cleanseth all, who - ev - er will, Praise God, it cleanseth me.

111   Thou Wilt Care for Me.

Words by LIZZIE EDWARDS.   Music by JNO. R. SWENEY.

1. Hope of end-less glo - ry, Source of joy di - vine,   Teach me how to
2. By thy grace up-hold me, Lest my feet should stray   From the light that
3. Je - sus, blessed Re - fuge, Safe in thee my rest;   There no harm can

praise thee, Bend my will to thine: Thou art pure and ho - ly, I am
shin - eth On my pil - grim way. Lean-ing on thy promise, Trusting
reach me, There no storms mo-lest. While my soul up-lift - ed, Views its

weak and frail; Yet I know thy promise Will not, cannot fail.
nought be-side; Where my faith is anchor'd, Let me still a - bide.
home a - bove, Sweet-ly comes the promise On the wings of love.

CHORUS.

Thou dost bid my wea - ry heart Leave its all with thee;

Thou hast said, and I be - lieve Thou wilt care for me.

Copyright, 1885, by Jno. R. SWENEY.

96

112 Refreshing. S. M.

Words by FANNY J. CROSBY.　　　　　　　　　Music by WM. J. KIRKPATRICK.

1. Come, Lord, and let thy pow'r　On each and all descend,　While
2. Come, Lord, and let thy pow'r　Each thought of self re-move;　And
3. Our wait - ing, longing eyes,　Are look - ing up to thee;　O
4. Come, Lord, thy pow'r a - lone,　The work of grace can do;　Now
5. Be ours, with fer-vent zeal,　Thy blood-stain'd cross to bear,　Till

gather'd in　thy ho - ly name,　Be - fore thy throne we bend.
may we feel　as ne'er be - fore　Thy pure and per - fect love.
may we, in　thy smiling face,　Our Fa - ther's glo - ry see.
let it con - se - crate to thee　Our hearts and lives a - new.
at　thy feet　we lay it down,　A crown of life to wear.

REFRAIN.

Re-fresh　our waiting souls,　Our fee - ble faith in - spire,　And

from thine al - tar touch our hearts With coals　of sa - cred fire.

113   We Come to be Blest.

Words by LIZZIE EDWARDS.   Music by JNO. R. SWENEY.

1. We come to be blest by our Saviour to-night; We meet at the gate of his love,
2. We come in his name to unburden our hearts, And ask for the grace that we need;
3. We come to be blest, and we firmly believe That Jesus this moment is near;
4. O Sav-iour, re-vive and in-spire us a-new The race set before us to run,

And fervently pray that our faith may behold A vis-ion from glory a-bove.
We come to acknowledge our sins of the past, And then his forgiveness to plead.
He tells us to ask, that our souls may receive The joy of his presence so dear.
Till, finish'd our course, thou shalt say to us all, My friends and my children, well
[done!

CHORUS.

Here, at the fountain, the clear, bright fountain, Whose waters are flowing for you and
[me,

We drink, and our sadness is turn'd into gladness; Praise God for the fountain of life so
[free.

114 Cleansed by the Blood.

Words by CARRIE M. WILSON. Music by WM. J. KIRKPATRICK.

1. I am jus-ti-fied by faith, And the peace of God is mine;
2. Now with bold-ness to his throne My be-liev-ing soul draws near;
3. O-ver-shadowed by his love, On my heart his name I bear;
4. I have con-se-cra-ted all To the ser-vice of the Lord;

I am jus-ti-fied by faith Thro' his right-eous-ness di-vine.
Ask-ing bless-ings at his hand, Not with trembling, nor with fear.
I can read my ti-tle clear, To a man-sion bright and fair.
I am lean-ing on his arm, And re-joic-ing in his Word.

CHORUS.

Cleans'd by the blood he shed to pur-chase me, Cleans'd by the blood to all e-ter-ni-ty; Cleans'd by the blood,

My song shall ev-er be, Cleans'd by the blood, hal-le-lu-jah!

115 Consecrate Me Now.

Words by FANNY J. CROSBY.

Music by JNO. R. SWENEY.

1. Con - se - crate me now, Je - sus, my Re-deem-er, Thine a - lone, and
2. Near - er would I live; near - er, ev - 'ry mo-ment, Let my faith with
3. When my work is done, when its cares are o - ver, When the gates of

thine for - ev - er, Lord, I would be; Pu - ri - fy my heart, all its dross
cloudless vis - ion mount up to thee; Pas-sive in thy hand, by thy will
yon - der cit - y joy - ful I see, Then before the throne, shouting hal-

D.S. Consecrate me now, Je - sus, my

Fine.

re - mov-ing, Let thine own E - ter - nal spir-it dwell with me.
di - rect - ed, Still in per - fect calm sub-mission hold thou me.
le - lu - jah, I will give the praise and glo-ry, Lord, to thee.

Re - deem-er, All I have is on the al - tar, all is thine.

CHORUS.

D.S.

O, my Saviour, come and bless me, Come in the fulness of love di - vine;

116 Saved by Grace. *

Words by Dr. H. L. GILMOUR.　　　　Music by WM. J. KIRKPATRICK.

1. When ling'ring on   life's sloping verge, As moments sink a - pace;
2. My Sav - iour shall be   with me then; Its floods shall not ef - face
3. I   long   to   see   him as   he   is, When done with earth's embrace;
4. I   soon shall hear the blood-wash'd throng, Throughout celestial   space,
5. Dash on,   old flood, thy surge is   vain; My Saviour's love-ly   face,

Each, passing, brings the Jor - dan near: A sin - ner sav'd by grace.
The peace - ful calm his pre - sence gives: A sin - ner sav'd by grace.
I   long   to know as   I   am known: A sin - ner sav'd by grace.
Re - peat the grand, tri-umph-ant song Of sin - ners sav'd by grace.
In death's dark vale, is bright to   me: A sin - ner sav'd by grace.

CHORUS.

Sav'd by grace,   sav'd by grace; Re - joice,   ye blood-bought race:

Pro-claim the ti - dings o'er and o'er, We're sav'd, we're sav'd by grace.

* *Dying Words of Bishop Simpson.*

117 All is Well.

Words by FRANK GOULD. Music by JNO. R. SWENEY.

1. Hark! I hear the in - vi - ta-tion, Come to Je - sus, he will save:
2. At the cross I leave my bur-den, All its heavy weight is o'er;
3. At the cross the faith that bore me Looks beyond with trusting eye,
4. Glo - ry, glo - ry, Je - sus saves me, O the words of love di - vine;

Lo! the crim-som tide is flowing, Now I plunge be-neath the wave.
Je - sus speaks to me so kind-ly, "Go in peace, and sin no more."
Where my Sav-iour's bow of promise Hangs a - loft in yon - der sky.
Glo - ry, glo - ry, now and ev - er, I am his, and he is mine.

CHORUS.

Glo - ry, glo - ry, Je - sus saves me, O my soul, his mer-cy tell;

Glo - ry, glo - ry, bless-ed rap-ture, Hal-le - lu - jah! all is well.

118   Behold what Manner of Love.

1 John, 3: 1.

Words by HENRIETTA E. BLAIR.   Music by WM. J. KIRKPATRICK.

1. Be - hold what manner of love, The Fa - ther on us hath bestow'd ; That
2. No more   in bondage of sin, Thro' grace we are free from the law ; And
3. Our souls bro't nigh unto God, While low   at his footstool we fall ; Ac -
4. O,   love,   O, wonderful love, Whose depth we can never ex-plore ; We

we by the Spirit, adopted his own, Should dwell in his blissful a-bode.
now to the fountain of love we may come, New life from its waters to draw.
cept-ed of Jesus, the son of his love, We praise the dear Father for all.
think of its grandeur, and shouting aloud, Its Au - thor and giver a - dore.

REFRAIN.

Be - hold what manner of love, Be - hold what manner of love The

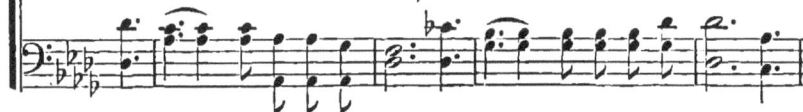

Father hath bestow'd up-on us, That we should be call'd the sons of God.

119 Go tell the World of His Love.

Words by Miss ABBIE MILLS.   Music by WM. J. KIRKPATRICK.

1. Heirs to the kingdom of Jesus, the Lord, Go tell the world of his love;
2. Think how he labor'd that we might have rest, Go tell the world of his love;
3. Plead with the lost ones to come while they may, Go tell the world of his love;

Publish the blessings that flow from his word, Go tell the world of his love:
Think how he suffer'd that we might be bless'd, Go tell the world of his love:
Je - sus is waiting, he'll save them to-day, Go tell the world of his love:

Love that has purchas'd redemption from sin, Love that makes happy the spirit within
Sav'd by his mercy, up-held by his care, Tell of the goodness we constantly share;
Love that is nearest when earth-joys are past, Lighting our pathway by clouds over-
[cast;

Fine.

Love that will help us our conquest to win, Go tell the world of his love.
Fill'd with his fulness, no longer forbear, Go tell the world of his love.
Love that will bring us to glory at last, Go tell the world of his love.

D.S. Cho. Heirs to the kingdom of Jesus, the Lord, Go tell the world of his love.

Go tell the World of His Love.

CHORUS. D.S.

Go tell the world, Go tell the world, Go tell the world of his love;

of his love;

(Dedicated to Wm. Taylor, Bishop of Africa.)

---

120   I am Trusting, Lord, in Thee.

Words by Rev. W. McDonald.   Music by Wm. G. Fischer.

1. I am com - ing to the cross; I'm poor, and weak, and blind;
2. Long my heart has sigh'd for thee; Long has e - vil dwelt with - in;

Cho.—I am trust - ing, Lord, in thee, Dear Lamb of Cal - va - ry;

I'm count-ing all but dross; I shall full sal - va - tion find.
Je-sus sweet-ly speaks to me,— I will cleanse you from all sin.

Humbly at thy cross I bow; Save me, Je - sus, save me now.

3 Here, I give my all to thee,
　Friends, and time, and earthly store,
Soul and body thine to be —
　Wholly thine—forevermore.

4 In the promises I trust;
　In the cleansing blood confide;
I am prostrate in the dust;
　I with Christ am crucified.

5 Jesus comes; he fills my soul!
　Perfected in love I am;
I am every whit made whole;
　Glory, glory to the Lamb!
　　(Chorus to 5th verse.)
Still I'm trusting, Lord, in thee,
　Dear Lamb of Calvary;
Humbly at thy cross I bow—
　Jesus saves me! saves me now!

105

121   Abiding.

Words by CHAS. B. J. ROOT.

Melody by D C. WRIGHT.
Arr. by R. K. CARTER.

1. A - bid - ing, oh, so wondrous sweet! I'm rest - ing at the Saviour's feet;
2. He speaks, and by his word is giv'n His peace, a rich foretaste of heav'n!
3. I live; not I through him a-lone, By whom the mighty work is done,
4. Now rest, my heart, the work is done, I'm sav'd thro' the E - ter - nal Son!

I trust in him, I'm sat - is-fied, I'm rest-ing in the cru - ci-fied!
Not as the world he peace doth give, 'Tis thro' this hope my soul shall live.
Dead to my-self, a - live to him, I count all loss his rest to gain.
Let all my pow'rs my soul employ, To tell the world my peace and joy.

CHORUS.

A - bid - - ing, a - bid - - ing, oh! so wondrous sweet!....

wondrous sweet!

A - bid-ing in him, I'm resting in him, oh! so wondrous sweet!

I'm rest - - ing, rest - - ing At the Sav-iour's feet.......

at his feet.

I'm resting in him, resting in him, At the Sav-iour's feet.......

122 Complaint. L. M.

PARMENTER.

1. Spare us, O Lord, a-loud we cry; Nor let our sun go down at noon:
Thy years are one eternal day, And must thy children die so soon?

2
I tremble, lest the wrath divine,
  Which bruises now my wretched soul,
Should bruise this wretched soul of mine
  Long as eternal ages roll.
3
I deprecate that death alone,
  That endless banishment from thee;

O save and give me to thy Son,
  Who trembled, wept, and bled for me.
4
Father, if I may call thee so,
  Regard my fearful heart's desire;
Remove this load of guilty woe,
  Nor let me in my sins expire.

---

123   STAY, THOU INSULTED SPIRIT, STAY.

1
Stay, thou insulted Spirit, stay,
  Though I have done thee such despite,
Nor cast the sinner quite away,
  Nor take thine everlasting flight.
2
Though I have steel'd my stubborn heart,
  And still shook off my guilty fears,
And vex'd and urg'd thee to depart,
  For many long rebellious years:

3
Though I have most unfaithful been,
  Of all who e'er thy grace received;
Ten thousand times thy goodness seen,
  Ten thousand times thy goodness griev'd;
4
Yet O! the chief of sinners spare,
  In honor of my great High Priest;
Nor in thy righteous anger swear
  T' exclude me from thy people's rest.

Seeking for Me.

E. E. HASTY.

1. Je-sus, my Saviour, to Beth-le-hem came; Born in a man-ger to
2. Je-sus, my Saviour, on Cal-va-ry's tree, Paid the great debt, and my
3. Je-sus, my Saviour, the same as of old, While I did wan-der a-
4. Je-sus, my Saviour, shall come from on high; Sweet is the promise as

sorrow and shame: Oh, it was wonderful, blest be his name, Seeking for me, for
soul he set free: Oh, it was wonderful, how could it be? Dy-ing for me, for
far from the fold, Gently and long he hath plead with my soul, Calling for me, for
wea-ry years fly: Oh, I shall see him descending the sky, Coming for me, for

for me, ...   for me, . . .

me,   Seeking for me,   Seeking for me,   Seeking for me,   Seeking for me:
me,   Dy-ing for me,   Dying for me,   Dy-ing for me,   Dying for me:
me,   Calling for me,   Calling for me,   Calling for me,   Calling for me:
me,   Coming for me,   Coming for me,   Coming for me,   Coming for me:

Oh, it was wonderful, blest be his name, Seeking for me, for   me.
Oh, it was wonderful, how could it be? Dy-ing for me, for   me.
Gen-tly and long he hath plead with my soul, Call-ing for me, for   me.
Oh, I shall see him descending the sky, Coming for me, for   me.

From "GOOD WILL," by per.

1. Je - sus, thine all-vic-to - rious love Shed in my heart a-broad;

Then shall my feet no long-er rove, Root - ed and fix'd in

Then shall my feet no long - - er
Then shall my feet no longer rove, Root-

Then shall my feet no long-er rove, Root-ed and fix'd in God.........

God.   Then shall my feet no long-er rove, Rooted and fix'd in God.

rove,   Then shall my feet no long-er rove, Rooted and fix'd in God.

- ed and fix'd in God,...............   Rooted and fix'd in God.

......   Then shall my feet no longer rove,

2 O that in me the sacred fire
    Might now begin to glow;
Burn up the dross of base desire,
    And make the mountains flow.

3 O that it now from heav'n might fall,
    And all my sins consume;
Come, Holy Ghost, for thee I call;
    Spirit of burning, come.

4 Refining fire, go through my heart;
    Illuminate my soul;
Scatter thy life through every part,
    And sanctify the whole.

5 My steadfast soul, from falling free,
    Shall then no longer move,
While Christ is all the world to me,
    And all my heart is love.

---

126   O JOYFUL SOUND OF GOSPEL GRACE!

1 O joyful sound of gospel grace!
    Christ shall in me appear;
I, even I, shall see his face,
    I shall be holy here.

2 The glorious crown of righteousness
    To me reached out I view: [seize
Conqueror through him, I soon shall
    And wear it as my due.

3 The promised land, from Pisgah's top,
    I now exult to see;

My hope is full, O glorious hope!
    Of immortality.

4 With me, I know, I feel, thou art;
    But this cannot suffice,
Unless thou plantest in my heart
    A constant paradise.

5 Come, O my God, thyself reveal,
    Fill all this mighty void:
Thou only canst my spirit fill;
    Come, O my God, my God!

127   The Sinner Invited.

Words and Music arr. by Rev. W. McDonald.

1. Sin - ner go, will you go To the high-lands of heav-en?
Where the storms nev - er blow, And the long sum-mer's giv - en:

D. C. And the leaves of the bow'rs In the breez-es are flit-ting.

Where the bright blooming flow'rs Are their o - dors e - mit-ting,

D.C.

2

Where the saints rob'd in white,
  Cleans'd in life's flowing fountain,
Shining beauteous and bright,
  They inhabit the mountain.
Where no sin nor dismay,
  Neither trouble nor sorrow,
Will be felt for a day,
  Nor be fear'd for the morrow.

3

He's prepared thee a home —
  Sinner, canst thou believe it?
And invites thee to come,
  Sinner, wilt thou receive it?
O come, sinner, come,
  For the tide is receding,
And the Saviour will soon
  And forever cease pleading.

128   Angels Hovering Round.

1. There are an - gels hov-'ring round, There are an - gels hov-'ring

round, There are an - - - gels, an - - - gels hov - 'ring round.

2 To carry the tidings home.
3 To the New Jerusalem.
4 Poor sinners are coming home.

5 And Jesus bids them come.
6 Let him that heareth, come.
7 We are on our journey home.

Concord. S. M.

HOLDEN, 1725.

Join in

1. Come ye that love the Lord, And let your joys be known ; Join in a song with sweet

ac - cord,... Join in a song with sweet accord, While ye surround the
a song with sweet accord, [throne.

2
The God that rules on high,
  That all the earth surveys,
That rides upon the stormy sky,
  And calms the roaring seas ;
This awful God is ours,
  Our Father and our Love:
He will send down his heav'nly pow'rs,
  To carry us above.

3
There we shall see his face,
  And never, never sin ;
There, from the rivers of his grace,
  Drink endless pleasures in :

Yea, and before we rise
  To that immortal state,
The thoughts of such amazing bliss
  Should constant joys create.

4
The men of grace have found
  Glory begun below :
Celestial fruit on earthly ground
  From faith and hope may grow :
Then let our songs abound,
  And every tear be dry :   [ground,
We're marching through Immanuel's
  To fairer world's on high.

130   I LOVE THY KINGDOM, LORD.

1
I love thy kingdom, Lord, —
  The house of thine abode, —
The church our blest Redeemer saved
  With his own precious blood.

2
I love thy Church, O God !
  Her walls before thee stand,
Dear as the apple of thine eye,
  And graven on thy hand.

3
For her my tears shall fall ;
  For her my prayers ascend ;

To her my cares and toils be given,
  Till toils and cares shall end.

4
Beyond my highest joy
  I prize her heavenly ways ;
Her sweet communion, solemn vows,
  Her hymns of love and praise.

5
Sure as thy truth shall last,
  To Zion shall be given
The brightest glories earth can yield,
  And brighter bliss of heaven.

131 Safe Within the Vail.

Rev. E. Adams.

J. M. Evans.

1. "Land a - head!" its fruits are waving O'er the hills of fade-less green;
2. Onward, bark! the cape I'm rounding; See, the bless-ed wave their hands;
3. There, let go the an-chor, riding On this calm and silvery bay;
4. Now we're safe from all temptation, All the storms of life are past;

And the liv - ing wa-ters lav-ing Shores where heav'nly forms are seen.
Hear the harps of God resounding From the bright im-mor-tal bands.
Sea - ward fast the tide is gliding, Shores in sunlight stretch a - way.
Praise the Rock of our Sal-va-tion, We are safe at home at last.

CHORUS.

Rocks and storms I'll fear no more, When on that e - ter-nal shore.

Drop the an - chor! furl the sail! I am safe with-in the vail!

132 He that goeth forth and weepeth.

J. E. H.
Music by J. E. HALL.

DUET. SOP. OR ALTO.

1. He that go - eth forth and weep-eth, Bear - ing precious seed,
2. He that go - eth forth and weep-eth, Trust-ing in the Lord,
3. He that go - eth forth and weep-eth, All a - glow with love,
4. He that go - eth forth and weep-eth, Christ he nev - er leaves,

TENOR.

Let him know that as he sow-eth To the sinner's need, So he'll reap.
Let him know that all he sow-eth Of the precious word, That he'll reap.
Oft-en-times, just while he sow-eth Hearts begin to move: So he'll reap.
Doubtless shall return re-joic-ing! Bringing home his sheaves, Thus, he'll reap.

CHORUS.

Sow-ing now,..... sow-ing now,..... But reaping by and by;

Sow-ing now, sow-ing now,

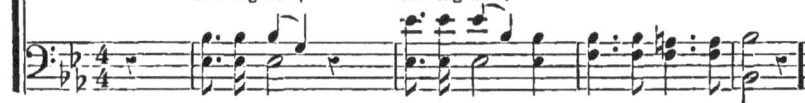

Weeping now,..... weeping now,..... Re - joic-ing by and by.

Weeping now, weeping now,

133
GRACE! 'TIS A CHARMING SOUND.

1 Grace! 'tis a charming sound,
  Harmonious to the ear;
Heaven with the echo shall resound,
  And all the earth shall hear.
    Chorus.
  I'm glad salvation's free,—
  I'm glad salvation's free,—
  Salvation's free for you and me,
  I'm glad salvation's free.

2 Grace first contrived a way
  To save rebellious man:

And all the steps that grace display,
  Which drew the wondrous plan.

3 Grace taught my roving feet
  To tread the heavenly road;
And new supplies each hour I meet,
  While pressing on to God.

4 Grace all the work shall crown
  Through everlasting days;
It lays in heaven the topmost stone,
  And well deserves our praise.
              PHILIP DODDRIDGE.

134
I LOVE TO TELL THE STORY.
(No. 44 in "BEULAH SONGS.")

1 I love to tell the story
  Of unseen things above;
Of Jesus and his glory,
  Of Jesus and his love!
I love to tell the story!
  Because I know its true;
It satisfies my longings
  As nothing else would do.

    Chorus.
I love to tell the story,
  'Twill be my theme in glory
To tell the old, old story
  Of Jesus and his love.

2 I love to tell the story!
  More wonderful it seems
Than all the golden fancies
  Of all our golden dreams.
I love to tell the story!
  It did so much for me!

And that is just the reason
  I tell it now to thee.

3 I love to tell the story!
  'Tis pleasant to repeat
What seems, each time I tell it,
  More wonderfully sweet.
I love to tell the story!
  For some have never heard
The message of salvation
  From God's own Holy Word.

4 I love to tell the story!
  For those who know it best
Seem hungering and thirsting
  To hear it like the rest.
And when, in scenes of glory,
  I sing the *New, New Song*,
'Twill be the *Old, Old Story*,
  That I have lov'd so long.
            MISS KATE HANKEY.

135
MY LIFE FLOWS ON IN ENDLESS SONG.
(No. 38 in "BEULAH SONGS.")

1 My life flows on in endless song,
  Above earth's lamentation;
I catch the sweet, though far off hymn
  That hails a new creation.
Through all the tumult and the strife,
  I hear the music ringing;
It finds an echo in my soul—
  How can I keep from singing?

2 What though my joys and comfort die?
  The Lord, my Saviour, liveth;
What though the darkness gather round?
  Songs in the night he giveth:

No storm can shake my inmost calm,
  While to that refuge clinging;
Since Christ is Lord of heav'n and earth,
  How can I keep from singing?

3 I lift my eyes; the cloud grows thin;
  I see the blue above it;
And day by day this pathway smooths,
  Since first I learned to love it:
The peace of Christ makes fresh my heart,
  A fountain ever springing;
All things are mine, since I am his,—
  How can I keep from singing?
            F. J. HARTLEY.

136 Where is my Soul to-night?

Words by Martha J. Lankton.　　　　　Music by Wm. J. Kirkpatrick.

1. Oft have I heard a voice that said, In tones that were soft and low,
2. Oft have I heard a warning voice That urg'd me to fly from sin;
3. Oft have I heard a ten-der voice, When troubled and care-op - press'd,
4. Oft have I heard a griev'd, sad voice, Entreating me o'er and o'er;

"Thy Saviour has lov'd, and loves thee yet, Then why wilt thou slight him so?"
To o - pen the door I long have clos'd, And welcome the Saviour in.
And then like a wea - ry child I sigh'd In Je-sus to find a rest.
And if I re-fuse to hear it now, Perhaps it will come no more.

CHORUS.

But where is my soul, where is my soul, Where is my soul to - night?

last v. O, Saviour, I yield, Saviour, I yield, Take thou my soul to - night.

That voice pleads on, pleads patiently on, But where is my soul to - night?

I now believe, and glad-ly receive Thy message of grace to - night.

"Glory, Hallelujah!" *

Rev. D. Williams.

1. On the moun - tain of vis - ion, what a glo - ry we be-hold!

A hundred years of vic - to - ry are tinging earth with gold; And the

glorious time is coming which the prophets long foretold. The Truth is marching on.

Chorus.—Glory, glory, hallelujah, &c.

2

For the glory of the Master, Wesley taught beyond the sea,
And preached the great salvation which delivers you and me;
And a million voices shout it,—"Redemption's full and free,"
    Salvation's rolling on.—Glory, glory, hallelujah, &c.

3

From the cabin on the prarie, from the vaulted city dome,
From the dark and briny ocean, where our sailor brothers roam,
We hear the glad rejoicing, like a happy harvest home.
    Salvation's rolling on. —Glory, glory, hallelujah, &c.

4

A hundred years of marching, and a hundred years of song,
The Conqueror advances, and the time will not be long
When he shall claim the heathen and overthrow the wrong.
    Our God is marching on.—Glory, glory, hallelujah, &c.

5

And when the war is over, with the saints forevermore,
On the blissful heights of Glory we will shout the battle o'er,
And in the Golden City we will join the Conqueror,
    Forever marching on.—Glory, glory, hallelujah, &c.

* The Chorus, "GLORY, HALLELUJAH," is so familiar, that the music need not be repeated.

Glory to His Name.

Words by Rev. Elisha Hoffman.　　　　　　Music by Rev. J. H. Stockton.

1. Down at the cross where my Saviour died, Down, where for cleansing from
2. I am so wondrously sav'd from sin: Je - sus so sweetly a -
3. Oh, precious fountain, that saves from sin, I am so glad I have
4. Come to this fountain, so rich and sweet; Cast thy poor soul at the

sin I cried; There to my heart was the blood applied: Glory to his
bides with-in; There at the cross where he took me in, Glory to his
en - ter'd in; There Je-sus saves me and keeps me clean, Glory to his
Saviour's feet; Plunge in to-day, and be made complete, Glory to his

CHORUS.

name. Glo - ry to his name. Glo - ry to his name.

There to my heart was the blood ap - plied, Glo - ry to his name.

139 He Saves to the Uttermost.

Words by CHAS. I. BUTLER.　　　　　　　　　　Music by JNO. R. SWENEY.

1. I was once far a-way from the Sav-iour, And as vile as a
2. But there in that lone-ly hour A voice sweetly
3. Ful-ly then trust-ed I in Je-sus, And oh, what a

sin-ner could be;...... I.... won-der'd if Christ, the Re-deem-er,
whisper'd to me, Say-ing, "Christ, the Re-deem-er, hath pow-er
joy came to me;...... My heart was filled with prais-es

Would save a poor sinner like me. I wan-dered on in the
To save a poor sinner like thee." I listen'd, and lo! 'twas the
For he sav'd a poor sinner like me. No long-er in dark-ness I'm

dark-ness, Not a ray of light could I see; And the
Sav-iour That was speak-ing so kind to me: I......
walk-ing, For the light is shin-ing on me; And

thought fill'd my heart with sadness, There's no hope for a sin-ner like me.
cried, "I'm the chief of sinners, Thou cans't save a poor sinner like me."
now un-to oth-ers I'm tell-ing How he sav'd a poor sinner like me.

140 The Healing Touch.

" When she heard of Jesus, came in the press behind, and touched his garment."—Mark 5 : 27

Words by Mrs. E. C. Ellsworth.   Music by Wm. J. Kirkpatrick.

1. An ea - ger, restless crowd drew near, And round the Sav - iour press'd ;
2. The mul - ti - tude, with cu - rious eyes, Just gaz'd up - on his face ;
3. Oh, near to Christ the man - y came, In that most fa - vor'd hour !
4. Of all who throng his courts to-day, Who shall re - ceive his word?

But *one*, with warm and lov - ing faith, His heal-ing pow'r con-fess'd.
But she glanc'd up with hope, and love, To feel his sav - ing grace.
But one stretch'd out the hand of faith, And touch'd his healing power.
Who shall reach forth with faith sin-cere, To touch the heal - ing Lord?

CHORUS.

She had touch'd the hem of his gar-ment, Trusting with all her soul ;

last v. Come and touch the hem of his garment, Trusting with all your soul ;

For ev - 'ry touch of the lov - ing Je - sus, Can make the wounded whole.

141   Dennis. S. M.

Arr. from H. G. NAGELI.

1. Fa - ther, I dare be - lieve Thee mer - ci - ful and true;

Thou wilt my guilt - y soul for - give, — My fall - en soul re - new.

2 Come then, for Jesus' sake,
   And bid my heart be clean;
An end of all my troubles make, —
   An end of all my sin.

3 I cannot wash my heart,
   But by believing thee,

And waiting for thy blood t' impart
   The spotless purity.

4 While at thy cross I lie,
   Jesus, thy grace bestow:
Now thy all cleansing blood apply,
   And I am white as snow!

---

142   O, COME AND DWELL IN ME.

1 O, come and dwell in me,
   Spirit of power within,
And bring the glorious liberty
   From sorrow, fear, and sin.

2 The seed of sin's disease,
   Spirit of health, remove, —
Spirit of finish'd holiness,
   Spirit of perfect love.

3 Hasten the joyful day
   Which shall my sins consume:

When old things shall be done away,
   And all things new become.

4 I want the witness, Lord,
   That all I do is right —
According to thy will and word —
   Well pleasing in thy sight.

5 I ask no higher state:
   Indulge me but in this,
And soon or later then translate
   To my eternal bliss.

---

143   A CHARGE TO KEEP I HAVE.

1 A charge to keep I have;
   A God to glorify:
A never-dying soul to save,
   And fit it for the sky.

2 To serve the present age,
   My calling to fulfil,
O, may it all my powers engage,
   To do my Master's will.

3 Arm me with jealous care,
   As in thy sight to live;
And oh, thy servant, Lord, prepare
   A strict account to give.

4 Help me to watch and pray,
   And on thyself rely;
Assured if I my trust betray,
   I shall forever die.

---

144   AND CAN I YET DELAY?

1 And can I yet delay
   My little all to give?
To tear my soul from earth away,
   For Jesus to receive?

2 Nay, but I yield, I yield!
   I can hold out no more:
I sink, by dying love compell'd,
   And own thee conqueror!

3 Though late, I all forsake, —
   My friends, my all resign:
Gracious Redeemer, take, oh! take
   And seal me ever thine.

4 Come, and possess me whole,
   Nor hence again remove;
Settle and fix my wavering soul
   With all thy weight of love.

145 Saved to the Uttermost.

W. J. K.

Music by W. J. KIRKPATRICK. By per.

1. Sav'd to the ut - ter-most: I am the Lord's; Je-sus, my Saviour, sal -
2. Sav'd to the ut - ter-most: Je-sus is near; Keeping me safe-ly, he
3. Sav'd to the ut - ter-most: this I can say, "Once all was darkness, but
4. Sav'd to the ut - ter-most: cheer-ful-ly sing Loud hal-le - lu - ias to

va - tion af - fords; Gives me his Spir - it a wit-ness with-in,
cast-eth out fear; Trusting his prom - is - es, how I am blest;
now it is day; Beau - ti - ful vis - ions of glo - ry I see,
Je-sus, my King! Ran-som'd and par - don'd, re - deem'd by his blood,

REFRAIN.

Whisp'ring of par - don, and sav-ing from sin. Sav'd, sav'd,
Lean - ing up - on him, how sweet is my rest.
Je - sus in bright - ness re - veal'd un - to me.
Cleans'd from un-right - eous-ness, glo - ry to God.

sav'd to the ut-ter-most: Sav'd, sav'd, by power divine; Sav'd, sav'd, I'm

sav'd to the ut - ter-most: Je - sus, the Saviour, is mine!

From "PRECIOUS SONGS."

146   Lovingly Bow to His Will.

Words by SALLIE M. SMITH.
SOLO OR DUET.

Music by JNO. R. SWENEY.

1. O, Christian, look up and be joyful; Look calmly, and nev-er re-pine:
2. O, Christian, look up and be joyful; The gloom that now mantles the sky,
3. Look up with more faith in his goodness, Look up with more trust in his word,
4. O, Christian, look up and be joyful; Whatev-er thy lot, be con-tent:

Tho' tri-als may sometimes oppress thee, O think what a Saviour is thine.
The clouds that are frowning above thee Will melt at the glance of his eye.
Look up with a per-fect submission, Then pray, and thy prayer will be heard.
For Je-sus, thy precious Re-deem-er, Be willing to spend and be spent.

CHORUS.   *rit.*

Look up, look up, o'er the turbulent sea; Lo, thy Redeemer is coming to thee!

a tempo.   *p*

O, let thy heart like the waters be still, Fervently, lovingly bow to his will.

147 WHEN I SURVEY THE WONDROUS CROSS.
(No. 106 in "Beulah Songs.")

1 When I survey the wondrous cross,
On which the Prince of Glory died,
My richest gain I count but loss,
And pour contempt on all my pride.

Chorus.
The cross, the cross, the precious cross,
The wondrous cross of Jesus;
From all our sin, its guilt and pow'r,
And every stain, it frees us.
Then I'm resting,
O, I'm resting at the cross;
Yes, I'm resting at the cross.

2 Forbid it, Lord, that I should boast,
Save in the death of Christ, my God;
All the vain things that charm me most,
I sacrifice them to his blood.

3 See, from his head, his hands, his feet,
Sorrow and love flow mingled down;
Did e'er such love and sorrow meet?
Or thorns compose so rich a crown?

4 Were the whole realm of nature mine,
That were a present far too small;
Love so amazing, so divine,
Demands my soul, my life, my all.

148 THE CROSS! THE BLOOD-STAINED CROSS!
(No. 50 in "Beulah Songs.")

1 The cross! the cross! the blood-stain'd
The hallow'd cross I see! [cross!
Reminding me of precious blood
That once was shed for me.

Chorus.
Oh, the blood, the precious blood!
That Jesus shed for me
Upon the cross, in crimson flood,
Just now by faith I see.

2 A thousand, thousand fountains spring
Up from the throne of God;
But none to me such blessings bring,
As Jesus' precious blood.

3 That priceless blood my ransom paid,
While I in bondage stood;
On Jesus all my sins were laid,
He sav'd me with his blood.

4 By faith that blood now sweeps away
My sins, as like a flood,
Nor lets one guilty blemish stay:
All praise to Jesus' blood.

5 This wondrous theme will best employ
My harp before my God,
And make all heaven resound with joy
For Jesus' cleansing blood.

Words, except 1st v. by Rev. W. McDonald.

149 I HEAR THE SAVIOUR SAY.
(No. 58 in "Beulah Songs.")

1 I hear the Saviour say,
Thy strength indeed is small;
Child of weakness, watch and pray,
Find in me thine all in all.

Chorus.
Jesus paid it all:
All to him I owe;
Sin had left a crimson stain,
He wash'd it white as snow.

2 O Lord, at last I find
Thy pow'r, and thine alone,
Can change this heart of mine,
And make it all thine own.

3 Then down beneath the cross
I lay my sin-sick soul;

Nothing I bring but dross,
Thy grace must make me whole.

4 I now in Christ abide —
In him is perfect rest;
Close sheltered in his side,
I am divinely blest.

5 When at my post I fall,
My ransom'd soul shall rise,
And "Jesus paid it all"
Shall rend the vaulted skies.

6 And when, in heav'n above,
At Jesus' feet I fall,
My song shall ever be —
Jesus has paid it all.

Arranged by Rev. W. McDonald.

150 MY BODY, SOUL, AND SPIRIT.
(No. 14 in "Beulah Songs.")

1 My body, soul, and spirit,
Jesus, I give to thee;
A consecrated offering,
Thine evermore to be.

Chorus.
My all is on the altar,
I'm waiting for the fire:
Waiting, waiting, waiting,
I'm waiting for the fire!

2 O Jesus, mighty Saviour,
I trust in thy great name;

I look for thy salvation,
Thy promise now I claim.

3 O let the fire, descending
Just now upon my soul,
Consume my humble offering,
And cleanse and make me whole.

4 I'm thine, O blessed Jesus,
Wash'd by thy cleansing blood;
Now seal me by thy Spirit,
A sacrifice to God.

MARY D. JAMES.

123

Behold the Bridegroom!

Words and Music by R. E. HUDSON. By per.

1. Are you ready for the Bridegroom when he comes, when he comes? Are you
2. Have your lamps trimm'd and burning When he comes, when he comes; Have your
3. We will all go out to meet him When he comes, when he comes; We will
4. We will chant al - le - lu - ias When he comes, when he comes; We will

ready for the Bridegroom When he comes, when he comes? Behold! he cometh! Be-
lamps trimm'd and burning When he comes, when he comes : He quickly cometh, he
all go out to meet him When he comes, when he comes ; He surely cometh! he
chant alleluias When he comes, when he comes ; Lo! now he cometh! Lo!

hold! he com-eth! Be rob'd and ready, for the Bride-groom comes.
quick-ly com-eth, O, soul! be ready when the Bride-groom comes.
sure - ly com-eth! We'll go to meet him, when the Bride-groom comes.
now he com-eth! Sing al - le - lu - ia! for the Bride-groom comes.

CHORUS.

Behold the Bridegroom, for he comes, Behold the Bridegroom, for he comes!
for he comes! for he comes,

Behold! he cometh! behold! he cometh! Be rob'd and ready, for the Bridegroom comes!

How firm à Foundation.

Arranged for this Work.

1. How firm a foundation, ye saints of the Lord, Is laid for your faith in his ex - cel-lent word; What more can he say, than to you he hath said, Ye who un-to Je - sus for refuge have fled?

2. In ev - 'ry con-di-tion, in sickness and health, In pov-er-ty's vale, or a - bound-ing in wealth, At home or a - broad, on the land, on the sea, As thy days may demand shall thy strength ever be.

3. Fear not, I am with thee; O be not dismay'd: I,— I am thy God, and will still give thee aid; I'll strengthen thee, help thee, and cause thee to stand, Up - held by my righteous Om-nip - o-tent hand.

4 When through the deep waters I call thee to go,
The rivers of woe shall not thee overflow;
For I will be with thee thy troubles to bless,
And sanctify to thee thy deepest distress.

5 When through fiery trials thy pathway shall lie,
My grace all sufficient shall be thy supply;
The flame shall not harm thee; I only design
Thy dross to consume, and thy gold to refine.

6 Even down to old age all my people shall prove
My constant, eternal, unchangeable love;
And when hoary hairs shall their temples adorn,
Like lambs they shall still on my bosom be borne.

7 The soul that on Jesus doth lean for repose,
I will not, I will not desert to his foes;
That soul, though all hell should endeavor to shake,
I'll never, no, never, no, never forsake.

153   Geistweit. S. M.

ISAAC WATTS.   WM. J. KIRKPATRICK.

1. The Lord my Shepherd is,   I shall be   well sup-plied;
2. He leads me to the place Where heav'nly   pas-ture grows;

Since he is mine, and I am his, What can I want be-side.
Where liv-ing wat-ers gently pass, And full sal-va-tion flows.

3 If e'er I go astray,
    He doth my soul reclaim,
And guides me in his own right way,
    For his most holy name.

4 While he affords his aid,
    I cannot yield to fear;   [shade,
Tho' I should walk thro' death's dark
    My Shepherd's with me there.

5 Amid surrounding foes,
    Thou dost my table spread;
My cup with blessings overflows,
    And joy exalts my head.

6 The bounties of thy love
    Shall crown my foll'wing days;
Nor from thy house will I remove,
    Nor cease to speak thy praise.

154   Meditation.   11s & 8s.

1. O thou, in whose presence my soul takes delight, On whom in affliction I call,

My comfort by day, and my song in the night, My hope, my salvation, my all!

2 Where dost thou, dear Shepherd, resort
    with thy sheep,
To feed them in pastures of love?
Say, why in the valley of death should
    I weep,
Or alone in this wilderness rove?

3 O why should I wander an alien from
    thee,
Or cry in the desert for bread:
Thy foes will rejoice when my sorrows
    they see,
And smile at the tears I have shed.

4 Ye daughters of Zion, declare, have you
    seen
The Star that on Israel shone?

Say, if in your tents my Beloved has
    been,
And where with his flocks he is gone.

5 He looks! and ten thousands of angels
    rejoice,
And myriads wait for his word:
He speaks! and eternity, filled with his
    voice,
Re-echoes the praise of the Lord.

6 Dear Shepherd, I hear, and will follow
    thy call;
I know the sweet sound of thy voice;
Restore and defend me, for thou art my
    all,
And in thee I will ever rejoice!

155   Like a River Glorious.

Words by FRANCES RIDLEY HAVERGAL.   Music by WM. J. KIRKPATRICK.

1. Like a riv-er glo-rious Is God's perfect peace, O-ver all vic - to - rious
2. Hidden in the hol-low Of his blessed hand, Never foe can fol-low,
3. Ev-'ry joy or tri - al Falleth from a - bove, Trac'd upon our di - al

In its bright in-crease. Perfect, yet it flow-eth Fuller every day;
Nev-er traitor stand. Not a surge of wor - ry, Not a shade of care,
By the Sun of Love. We may trust him sole-ly, All for us to do;

Perfect, yet it grow-eth Deeper all the way. *CHORUS.* Stay'd up-on Je - ho-vah,
Not a blast of hur - ry Touch the spirit there.
They who trust him wholly, Find him wholly true.

Hearts are truly blest, Finding, as he promis'd, Perfect peace and rest.

156   Wait for the Blessing.

Words by FANNY J. CROSBY.

Music by JNO. R. SWENEY.

1. A cloud from the sea is ris-ing, And tho' it may seem so small,
2. A cloud o'er the sky is spreading, What joy it will bring to all;
3. Our souls for the rain are thirsting, And Jesus will hear our call;
4. Oh! cloud from the sea a - ris-ing, Oh! cloud that may seem so small;

If still we in prayer con - tin - ue, The show'r that we ask will fall.
For soon it will burst up - on us, The show'r that we ask will fall.
Al - read-y the drops de-scend-ing, Proclaim that the show'r will fall.
We hail thy di - vine re-fresh-ing, And welcome thy drops that fall.

CHORUS.

We'll wait for the blessing that surely will come, As surely as God has spoken;

We'll wait for the blessing, and trust in the Lord, Whose promise can never be broken!

A Stronger Faith.

Words by MARTHA J. LANKTON.　　　Music by WM. J. KIRKPATRICK.

1. A stronger faith, dear Saviour, A firm-er, deep-er love, We need while
2. A stronger faith, dear Saviour, More love to do thy will; And where thy
3. A stronger faith, dear Saviour, A per-fect trust in thee; A faith in
4. A faith that, firm and steadfast, Beholds thy constant light; But sees thy

CHORUS.

on the jour-ney To reach our home a - bove. To us, O Lord, that
voice would lead us, Thy steps to fol-low still.
ev - 'ry tri - al Our Father's hand to see.
smile the clearest Thro' clouds of darkest night.

faith impart, On us that love be - stow; Till, borne a - way, on wings we

rise, Where joys e - ter - nal flow. Where joys e - ter - nal flow.

Christ For Me.

Music by W. H. DOANE.

1. { My heart is fix'd, E - ter-nal God, Fix'd on thee, fix'd on thee!
And my im-mor-tal choice is made, (*Omit*) .... Christ for

D. C. And while I breathe I mean to sing, (*Omit*) .... Christ for

Fine.

me, Christ for me. He is my Prophet, Priest and King, Who did for me salvation

me, Christ for me. [bring.

D C

2
Let others boast of heaps of gold,
Christ for me, Christ for me;
His riches never can be told,
Christ for me, Christ for me!
Your gold will waste and wear away,
Your honor perish in a day —
My portion never can decay;
Christ for me, Christ for me!

3
In pining sickness, or in health,
Christ for me, Christ for me;
In deepest poverty or wealth,
Christ for me, Christ for me!
And in that all important day,
When I the summons must obey,
And pass from this dark world away,
Christ for me, Christ for me!

4
At home, abroad, by night and day,
Christ for me, Christ for me;
Whether I preach, or sing, or pray,
Christ for me, Christ for me!

Him first and last, him all day long,
My hope, my solace and my song,
Convince me if you think I'm wrong,
Christ for me, Christ for me!

5
Now who can sing my song and say
Christ for me, Christ for me;
My light and truth, my life and way,
Christ for me, Christ for me!
Can you, oh! man and woman there,
With furrowed cheeks and silvery hair,
Now from your inmost soul declare,
Christ for me, Christ for me!

6
Can you, young men and maidens, say,
Christ for me, Christ for me?
Him will I love, and him obey,
Christ for me, Christ for me?
Then here's my heart, and here's my hand
To form a happy singing band,
And shout aloud through all the land
Christ for me, Christ for me!

The Rifted Rock.

L. T. H.

Music by Rev R. LOWRY.

1. In the Rift - ed Rock I'm rest-ing, Sure and safe from all   a - larm;
2. Many a storm - y sea I've travers'd, Many a tempest-shock have known;
3. Yet I now have found a ha - ven, Nev-er mov'd by tempest-shock,

Storms and bil - lows have u - ni - ted, All   in vain, to do   me harm:
Have been driv - en, with-out an - chor, On   the bar - ren shores, and lone.
Where my soul is safe for-ev - er, In   the bless-ed Rift - ed Rock.

In the Rift - ed Rock I'm rest-ing, Surf is dash-ing at   my feet;

Cho.—In the Rift - ed Rock I'm rest-ing, Sure and safe from all   a - larm;

D.S. for Chorus.

Storm-clouds dark are o'er me hovering, Yet my rest is   all com-plete.

Storms and bil-lows have u - ni - ted, All   in vain, to do me harm.

160   Almost.

Words by Mrs. O. F. WALTON.

Music by JNO. R. SWENEY.

1. So near the door, and the door stood wide? Close to the port, but
2. Lord, help me trust in thy word to - day, That thou art the Light, the
3. Saviour, I come, I cry un-to thee, O let not these words be

not in - side! Near to the fold, yet not with - in,
Truth, the Way. Now as I come, with my load of sin, The
true of me, I want to come to the point to - day. O

Al - most re - solved to give up sin! Al-most persuaded to
door be - ing o - pen, O help me step in. How sad the thought that for
suf - fer me not to turn a - - way; Give me no rest, till my

count the cost, Al-most a christian, and yet lost?
me, at last, The door should be shut, and mer - cy past!
soul shall be Within the Refuge,— safe with thee.

161 I'm Resting in the Crucified.

" Ye shall find rest unto your souls."—Matt. 11: 29.

F. A. B. Music by F. A. BLACKMER.

1. The Cru - ci - fied of Cal - va - ry Has ta - ken all my load of sin;
2. Wea - ry and sad I wander'd, long Oppress'd with burdens hard to bear;
3. Oh, what a resting-place is this, And ref - uge for the wea - ry soul,
4. Se - cure from ev'ry foe am I, While rest-ing in the Cru - ci - fied:

Has cleans'd my heart from ev'ry stain, And brought the glorious fullness in.
But when the Cru-ci-fied I sought, I found sweet rest and solace there.
Where sin's wild ocean cannot drown, Tho' near its threat'ning billows roll!
Here is a calm and safe re-treat, And here I ev - er would a - bide.

CHORUS.

The Cru - ci - fied of Cal - va - ry, I'm sweet-ly resting in the Cru - ci - fied:

He saves me now, and all the time I'm sweetly resting in the Cru-ci-fied.

162 White as Snow.

Words by Rev. W. McDonald.

Arranged by Rev. W. McD.

Ad lib.

1. Ah, ma-ny years my burden'd heart Has sigh'd, has long'd to know
2. I heard the saints in rap-ture tell, How much a soul may know
3. I came to Je-sus sick and vile, That I this grace might know;
4. He cast on me a look of love, Such as no words can show;
5. I'll tell to ev-'ry saint I meet, To sin-ners high and low,
6. And when to that bright world a-bove, My raptur'd soul shall go,

The vir-tue of my Saviour's blood, That wash-es white as snow.
Of Je-sus' precious cleansing blood, That wash-es white as snow.
And trusted in his precious blood To wash me white as snow.
I felt with-in my very soul He wash'd me white as snow.
That, trusting in the Saviour's blood, It wash-es white as snow.
My song shall be—The precious blood, Still wash-es white as snow.

CHORUS.

There is pow'r in Je-sus' blood, There is pow'r in Je-sus'

blood, There is pow'r in Je-sus' blood To wash me white as snow.

163   The Precious Name.

Words by Mrs. LYDIA BAXTER.   Music by W. H. DOANE.

1. Take the name of Je - sus with you, Child of sor-row and of woe —
2. Take the name of Je - sus ev - er, As a shield from ev-'ry snare ;
3. Oh! the precious name of Je - sus; How it thrills our souls with joy,
4. At the name of Je - sus bow-ing, Fall-ing prostrate at his feet,

It will joy and comfort give you, Take it then where'er you go.
If temptations round you gath - er, Breathe that holy name in prayer.
When his lov-ing arms re-ceive us, And his songs our tongues employ.
King of kings in heav'n we'll crown him, When our journey is com-plete.

CHORUS.

Precious name,   O how sweet!   Hope of earth and joy of heav'n.

Precious name,   O how sweet!

Precious name,   O how sweet! Hope of earth and joy of heav'n.

Precious name, O how sweet, how sweet,

164 Wondrous Glory.

Words by SALLIE M. SMITH. Music by JNO. R. SWENEY.

1. On the mount of wondrous glo - ry, Borne a - loft by faith we stand,
2. On the mount of wondrous glo - ry, Where so oft 'tis ours to be,
3. On the mount of wondrous glo - ry, Where he bids me come and rest,
4. If on earth our souls are hon - or'd With such vis-ions of de - light,

While we drink the crys-tal wa - ters Flow-ing down from E-den's land.
In the brightness of his presence, Christ, our Lord, reveal'd we see.
Je - sus spreads a feast be - fore us, Making each a wel-come guest.
Who can tell our heights of rap - ture, When our faith is lost in sight.

CHORUS.

How the heart........ its toil for - gets, In the
How the heart, its toil for-gets,

joy.......... we there be - hold; In the ful - - -
In the joy we there be - hold, there be-hold, In the

- - - ness of his love, That is bet - ter felt than told.
ful - ness of his love, of his love,

165 Under His Wings.

Words by JAMES NICHOLSON.

Music by ASA HULL.

1. In God I have found a re-treat, Where I can se-cure-ly a-bide;
2. I dread not the ter-ror by night, No ar-row can harm me by day;
3. The pes-ti-lence walking a-bout, When darkness has set-tled a-broad,
4. The wasting destruction at noon, No fear-ful for-bo-ding can bring;
5. A thousand may fall at my side, And ten thousand at my right hand;

No refuge nor rest so complete, And here I in-tend to re-side.
His shadow has covered me quite, My fears he has driven a-way.
Can nev-er com-pel me to doubt The presence and power of God.
With Je-sus, my soul doth commune, His per-fect sal-vation I sing.
A-bove me his wings are spread wide, Beneath them in safe-ty I stand.

CHORUS.

Oh, what com-fort it brings, As my soul sweet-ly sings:

I am safe from all dan-ger While un-der his wings.

166   O save me at the Cross.

Words by Fanny J. Crosby, 1874.

Arr. by H. P. Main.

1. Lov - ing Sav-iour, hear my cry, hear my cry, hear my cry,
   I have sinn'd, but thou hast died, thou hast died, thou hast died:

Trembling, to thy arms I fly, O save me at the cross.
In thy mer - cy let me hide, O save me at the cross.

CHORUS.

Dear Je - sus, re - ceive me, No more would I grieve thee,

Now, bless-ed Re - deem - er, O save me at the cross.

2
Though I perish, ‖ I will pray,‖
Thou of life the living way,
    O save me at the cross.
Thou hast said thy ‖ grace is free,‖
Have compassion, Lord, on me,
    O save me at the cross.—*Cho.*

3
Wash me in thy ‖ cleansing blood,‖
Plunge me now beneath the flood,
    O save me at the cross.
Only faith will ‖ pardon bring,‖
In that faith to thee I cling,
    O save me at the cross. —*Cho.*

167   The Solid Rock.

Words by E. Mote.   Music by Wm. B. Bradbury.

1. { My hope is built on nothing less Than Jesus' blood and righteousness ;
{ I dare not trust the sweetest frame, But wholly lean on Jesus' name :

CHORUS.

On Christ, the sol - id Rock, I stand ; All other ground is sinking sand,

All other ground is sinking sand.

2 When darkness seems to veil his face,
I rest on his unchanging grace ;
In every high and stormy gale,
My anchor holds within the vale.

3 His oath, his covenant and blood,
Support me in the whelming flood ;
When all around my soul gives way,
He then is all my hope and stay.

168   Happy Day.

1. { O, hap-py day, that fix'd my choice On thee my Saviour and my God !
{ Well may this glowing heart re-joice, And tell its raptures all a-broad.

2
O happy bond, that seals my vows
To him who merits all my love ;
Let cheerful anthems fill his house,
While to that sacred shrine I move.
Cho.—Happy day, &c.

3
'Tis done, the great transaction's done ;
I am my Lord's, and he is mine :
He drew me, and I followed on,
Charm'd to confess the voice divine.
Cho.—Happy day, &c.

4
Now rest, my long-divided heart,
Fix'd on this blissful centre, rest,
Nor ever from thy Lord depart,
With him of every good possess'd.
Cho.—Happy day, &c.

6
High Heav'n, that heard the solemn vow,
That vow renewed shall daily hear,
Till in life's latest hour I bow,
And bless in death a bond so dear.
Cho.—Happy day, &c.

169   The Prince of my Peace.

Words by Rev. W. F. CRAFTS.

Music by W. G. FISCHER. By per.

1. I stand all bewildered with wonder, And gaze on the ocean of love;
2. I struggled and wrestled to win it, The blessing that setteth me free;
3. He laid his hand on me and heal'd me, And bade me be every whit whole;
4. The Prince of my peace is now passing, The light of his face is on me;

And o-ver its waves to my spir-it Comes peace, like a heavenly dove.
But when I had ceas'd from my struggles, His peace Jesus gave unto me.
I touch'd but the hem of his gar-ment, And glory came thrilling my soul.
But listen, be-lov-ed, he speaketh: "My peace I will give unto thee."

REFRAIN.

The cross now covers my sins; The past is under the blood;

I'm trusting in Jesus for all; My will is the will of my God.

170 The Crimson Stream.

Words by Rev. W. J. STEVENSON.　　　Music by S. B. ELLENBERGER. By per.

1. I stand be-side the crimson stream That flows from Cal-vary's mount,
2. The blood of Christ a - lone will save From guilt, and fear, and care;
3. I claim the promised blessing now, Free-dom from ev - 'ry sin:
4. I sink in - to the crimson stream, Christ's blood is now ap - plied:

And long to wash a - way all sin, With-in its cleansing fount.
His blood will sweetly pu - ri - fy, When sought in earnest prayer.
The pow'r to lead a ho - ly life, With Christ in God, shut in.
I rise a - gain, re-deem'd by him, And wholly pu - ri - fied.

CHORUS.

Now wash me, now wash me, And cleanse me from sin;

Now wash me, now wash me, And I shall be clean.

171 The Fountain of Mercy.

Words by H. Q. WILSON.　　　　　　　　　Music by ASA HULL.

1. 'Twas Je-sus, my Saviour, who died on a tree, To o-pen a
Cho.—For the Li-on of Ju-dah shall break ev-'ry chain, And give us the
[has bro-ken]　　　　　　　　　　[gives]

fountain for sin-ners like me; His blood is that fountain, which
vic-t'ry a-gain and a-gain; For the Li-on of Ju-dah shall
[has]

rit. un poco.　D.C.

par-don be-stows, And cleanses the foulest wher-ev-er it flows.
break ev-'ry chain, And give us the vic-t'ry a-gain and a-gain.
[broken]　　　　　　　[gives]

2 And when I was willing with all things to part,
He gave me my bounty,—his love in my heart;
So now I am joined with the conquering band
Who are marching to glory at Jesus' command.
Chorus.—For the Lion of Judah, etc.

3 Though round me the storms of adversity roll,
And the waves of destruction encompass my soul,
In vain this frail vessel the tempest shall toss:
My hopes rest secure on the blood of the cross.
Chorus.—For the Lion of Judah, etc.

4 And when the last trumpet of judgment shall sound,
And wake all the nations that sleep in the ground,
Then, when heaven and earth shall be melting away,
I'll sing of the blood of the cross in that day.
Chorus.—For the Lion of Judah, etc.

5 And when with the ransomed by Jesus, my head,
From fountain to fountain I then shall be led;
I'll fall at his feet and his mercy adore,
And sing of the blood of the cross evermore.
Chorus.— For the Lion of Judah, etc.

O, how I Love Him.

W. J. K.

WM. J. KIRKPATRICK.

1. I have found a precious Friend, On whose Word my hopes de-pend:
2. When beneath Je - ho - vah's frown My crush'd heart was sinking down,
3. When I struggled all in vain, Peace and par-don to ob-tain,
4. When the tempter's pow'r assail'd, And my courage well nigh fail'd,
5. When I sought to know his will, Ev - 'ry pur-pose to ful - fil,

Je - sus, Saviour, Brother too, Ev - er faithful, ev - er true.
Je - sus heard my plaintive cry, Came and brought Salva - tion nigh.
Je - sus came to my re - lief, Bore my weight of sin and grief.
Je - sus brought his ar - mor bright, Made me Vic - tor by his might.
Je - sus took me by the hand, Led me up to Beu - lah Land.

CHORUS.

O, how I love him, O, how I love him, O, how I love him, My

best, my dear - est Friend!

6 Now, when waves of care and woe
Come my soul to overthrow,
Jesus in his arms of love
Lifts me, bears me far above.

7 Now I'll magnify his name,
His great goodness I'll proclaim;
In my heart he comes to stay,—
Keeps me, saves me, day by day.

173 Fill Me Now.

Words by E. H. STOKES, D. D. Music by JNO. R. SWENEY.

1. Hov-er o'er me, Ho-ly Spir-it; Bathe my trembling heart and brow;

D.S. Fill me with thy hallow'd presence, Come, oh, come and fill me now.

CHORUS.

Fill me now, fill me now, Je-sus, come and fill me now:

2 Thou can'st fill me, gracious Spirit,
  Though I cannot tell thee how;
But I need thee, greatly need thee;
  Come, oh, come and fill me now.

3 I am weakness, full of weakness;
  At thy sacred feet I bow;

Blest, divine, eternal Spirit,
  Fill with pow'r, and fill me now.

4 Cleanse and comfort, bless and save me;
  Bathe, oh, bathe my heart and brow;
Thou art comforting and saving,
  Thou art sweetly filling now.

174 COME, THOU FOUNT OF EVERY BLESSING.

1 Come, thou fount of every blessing,
  Tune my heart to sing thy grace;
Streams of mercy never ceasing,
  Call for songs of loudest praise.

2 Teach me some melodious sonnet,
  Sung by flaming tongues above;
Praise the mount—I'm fixed upon it—
  Mount of thy redeeming love!

3 Here I'll raise mine Ebenezer;
  Hither by thy help I'm come:
And I hope, by thy good pleasure,
  Safely to arrive at home.

4 Jesus sought me, when a stranger,
  Wandering from the fold of God;
He, to rescue me from danger,
  Interposed his precious blood.

175 Remember Me. C. M.

1. { Come, Ho-ly Ghost, in-spire our songs With thine im-mor-tal flame; }
   { En-large our hearts, unloose our tongues To praise the Sav-iour's name. }

Cho. { Re-mem-ber me, re-mem-ber me, Dear Lord, re-mem-ber me, }
       { Re-mem-ber, Lord, thy dy-ing groans, And then re-mem-ber me. }

176 Coming to Jesus.

Words by Rev. W. H. BURRELL. Music by JNO. R. SWENEY. By per.

1. With my sin-wounded soul, To be made ful-ly whole. And thy per-fect sal-va-tion to see, With my heart all a-glow, To be wash'd white as snow, I am coming, dear Sav-iour, to thee.

2. Oh, how long I have tried To re-sist na-ture's tide! All in vain have I sigh'd to be free; In my-self all undone,'Neath the waves sink-ing down, I am coming, dear Sav-iour, to thee.

3. I, thy promise be-lieve, That in thee I shall live, Thro' thy blood shed so free-ly for me; To ob-tain a pure heart, And se-cure the good part, I am coming, dear Sav-iour, to thee.

4. To be thine, wholly thine, Precious Saviour di-vine, With my all con-se-cra-ted to thee; To be kept ev-'ry hour, By thy love's wondrous pow'r, I am coming, dear Sav-iour, to thee.

REFRAIN.

I am coming, dear Saviour, to thee, I am coming, dear Saviour, to thee, With my heart all aglow, To be wash'd white as snow, I am coming, dear Saviour, to thee.

177   Still out of Christ.

Words by H. E. BLAIR.   Music by WM. J. KIRKPATRICK.

1. Still out of Christ, when so oft he has call'd you, Why will you longer re-
2. Still out of Christ, and the moments so precious, Night is approaching, O
3. Still out of Christ, yet for you there is mercy, If you are willing to
4. Still out of Christ, and the love he has promis'd, How you are longing that

fuse to be-lieve? What can you hope from the world or its pleasure?
what will you do? Still out of Christ, yet there's room at the fountain,
turn from your sin ; Yon-der he stands, at the door of sal-va-tion,
love to re-ceive : Haste, where the star of your faith is di-rect-ing,

REFRAIN.

How can you trust them, when both will deceive? Come, come to Je-sus,
Free are its wat-ers, and flow-ing for you.
Wait-ing to par-don and wel-come you in.
Haste, and this mo-ment re-pent and be-lieve.

weary, heavy-hearted, Come, come to Je-sus, while you may ; Now he is

Still out of Christ. Concluded.

wait-ing, waiting to receive you, Hark, he is call-ing you to-day.

178   **Angelus.**   7s & 6s.

1. { I could not do with-out thee, O Sav - iour of the lost! }
   { Whose precious blood re - deem'd me At such tre - men-dous cost. }

Thy right-eous-ness, thy par - don, Thy pre - cious blood must be

My on - ly hope 'and com - fort, My glo - ry and my plea.

2 I could not do without thee,
   I cannot stand alone;
I have no strength or goodness,
   No wisdom of my own;
But thou, beloved Saviour,
   Art all in all to me;
And weakness will be power,
   If leaning hard on thee.

3 I could not do without thee,
   For oh! the way is long,
And I am often weary,
   And sigh replaces song.
How could I do without thee?
   I do not know the way;
Thou knowest and thou leadest,
   And wilt not let me stray.

179   'Tis with the Righteous well.

Arranged for this Work.

1. On ev-'ry sun-ny mountain, In ev-'ry gloomy dell, What-e'er the
2. What words of ho-ly comfort! Their sweetness who can tell? With-in the
3. Tho' dripping clouds may gather, And grief the bosom swell, The trust-ing
4. And when the strife is o-ver, And hush'd the solemn knell, With-in the

CHORUS.

robe that wraps the heart, 'Tis with the righteous well. 'Tis well, 'tis well, 'tis
vail, and o'er the flood, 'Tis with the righteous well.
heart will ev-er sing,—'Tis with the righteous well.
gates, around the throne, 'Tis with the righteous well.

'tis well,   'tis well,

with the righteous well; In pleasure's light, and sor-row's night, 'Tis

1.   2.   *Ritard.*

with the righteous well;   and sorrow's night, 'Tis with the righteous well.

180 God's Promises.

2 Peter, 1: 4.

Words by Mrs. MARY D. JAMES

Music by WM. J. KIRKPATRICK.

1. O, glo - rious prom-is - es of God! Each one a price-less gem!
2. No fail - ure in his prom-is - es, But stead-fast, firm and sure;
3. Be - liev - ing them, the Spir-it's pow'r Re - news and pu - ri - fies,

The rich - est diamonds of the earth Are naught compar'd to them.
The Word of our unchanging God For - ev - er shall en - dure.
Thro' Christ's all-cleansing, precious blood, Our per - fect sac - ri - fice.

Most bless-ed boon to mor-tals giv'n, To cheer life's dreary way;
Tho' heav'n and earth shall pass a - way, And all we love may die,
O, glo - rious leg - a - cy of heav'n, So rich, so vast and free,

Fine.

Bright lights let down to show the path To ev - er - last - ing day.
God's prom-is - es to us re - main,—On these we may re - ly.
These pre-cious prom-is - es di - vine, Se - curing all to me.

D.S. these I'm rich, with these se - cure, While endless a - ges roll.

CHORUS.

D.S.

Sweet promises! God's promises! Dear treasures of my soul; With

181 Mercy is Boundless and Free.

Words by HENRIETTA E. BLAIR.　　　　Music by WM. J. KIRKPATRICK. By per.

1. Thanks be to Je-sus, his mer-cy is free; Mer-cy is free,
2. Why on the mountains of sin wilt thou roam? Mer-cy is free,
3. Think of his goodness, his pa-tience and love; Mer-cy is free,
4. Yes, there is par-don for all who be-lieve; Mer-cy is free,

Refrain.—Je-sus, the Sav-iour, is look-ing for thee, look-ing for thee,

mer-cy is free: Sin-ner, that mer-cy is flow-ing for thee,
mer-cy is free: Gent-ly the Spir-it is calling, "Come home,"
mer-cy is free: Plead-ing thy cause with his Father a-bove,
mer-cy is free: Come and this mo-ment a blessing re-ceive,

look-ing for thee; Lov-ing-ly, ten-der-ly call-ing for thee,

Fine.

Mer-cy is boundless and free. If thou art willing on
Mer-cy is boundless and free. Thou art in darkness, O,
Mer-cy is boundless and free. Come and re-pent-ing, O,
Mer-cy is boundless and free. Je-sus is wait-ing, O,

Call-ing and look-ing for thee.

him to be-lieve, Mer-cy is free, mer-cy is free.
come to the light, Mer-cy is free, mer-cy is free.
give him thy heart, Mer-cy is free, mer-cy is free.
hear him pro-claim Mer-cy is free, mer-cy is free.

Mercy is Boundless and Free. Concluded.

D.C. Refrain.

Life ev-er-last-ing thy soul may receive, Mercy is boundless and free.
Jesus is waiting, he'll save you to-night, Mercy is boundless and free.
Grieve him no longer, but come as thou art, Mercy is boundless and free.
Cling to his mercy, believe on his name, Mercy is boundless and free.

182 Rejoicing Evermore.

Music by R. E. HUDSON. By per.

1. Tho' troubles as-sail, and dan - gers affright, Tho' friends should all
2. The birds, with-out barn or storehouse are fed; From them let us
3. When Sa-tan ap-pears to stop up our path, And fills us with
4. He tells us we're weak,—our hope is in vain; The good that we

Chorus.—Yes, I will re-joice, re-joice in the Lord. Yes, I will re-

fail, and foes all u-nite, Yet one thing secures us, whatever be -
learn to trust for our bread: His saints what is fit-ting shall ne'er be de-
fears, we tri - umph by faith; He cannot take from us, (though oft he has
seek we ne'er shall ob-tain: But when such suggestions our graces have

joice, re-joice in the Lord. Yes, I will re-joice, re-joice in the

tide, The prom-ise as-sures us,—The Lord will pro - vide.
nied, So long as 'tis written,—The Lord will pro - vide.
tried) The heart-cheer-ing promise,—The Lord will pro - vide.
tried, This answers all questions,—The Lord will pro - vide.

Lord, Will joy in the God of my sal-va - tion.

183 There's Music in my Soul!

Words by Rev. HENRY BURTON.　　　　　　Music by JOSHUA GILL.

1. The world is full of singing, I hear it everywhere; The flow'rs their bells are
2. My heart was fond of sighing, With just some breaks of song, As self was ev - er
3. My life was full of sadness, Of overweighting care; But now the "oil of
4. And so my heart keeps clinging To the dear Master's Word; And it is al - ways

ring-ing Out on the scented air: And up a - bove, around me, The
try - ing To make its weakness strong; But now in him con-fid-ing, His
gladness" Has turn'd to praise the prayer: And so I keep pur-su-ing, And
sing-ing, Just like a spring-time bird: I know not what the harps be, Where

si - lent anthems roll : The glorious Lord has found me, There's music in my soul!
Word has made me whole, And e'er in Christ abiding, There's music in my soul!
pressing t'ward the goal ; But praying, waiting, doing, There's music in my soul!
heav'nly anthems roll ; I know that heav'n is near me, There's music in my soul!

CHORUS.

The blood of Christ is flow-ing, Its waves a-round me roll;

My heart with love is glow-ing, There's mu - sic in my soul!

The Pilgrim Company.

Arranged by Rev. W. McDonald.

1. What poor de-spi-sed com-pa-ny Of trav-el-ers are these,
Chorus.—I had rath-er be the least of them, Who are the Lord's a - lone,
2. Ah! these are of a roy-al line, All children of a King!
3. Why do they then ap-pear so mean? And why so much de-spis'd?

D.C. for Chorus.

Who walk in yon-der nar-row way, A - long that rug-ged maze?
Than wear a roy-al di - a-dem, And sit up - on a throne.
Heirs of im-mor-tal crowns di-vine, And lo! for joy they sing.
Be - cause of their rich robes un-seen The world is not ap-pris'd.

And sit up - on a throne, And sit up - on a throne;

Than wear a roy-al di - a-dem, And sit up - on a throne.

4	6
But some of them seem poor, distress'd,	But why keep they the narrow road,
And lacking daily bread:	That rugged thorny maze?
Ah! they're of boundless wealth possess'd,	Why, that's the way their Leader trod;
With heavenly manna fed.	They love and keep his ways.
5	**7**
Why do they shun the pleasing path	What, is there then no other road
That worldlings love so well?	To Salem's happy ground?
Because it is the way to death:	Christ is the only way to God:
The open road to hell.	None other can be found.

185 Let me Sing.

Words by FANNY J. CROSBY.　　　　　　　　Music by JNO. R. SWENEY.

1. Let me sing, let me sing, O my Sav-iour, of thee, Let me pub-lish a -
2. Let me sing, let me sing of the joy that is mine, Of thy won-der - ful
3. Let me sing, let me sing like a bird in its nest, How thy sweet, gentle
4. Let me sing, let me sing till my jour-ney is o'er, Let me sing till on

broad thy re - demp-tion so free: Of the an - guish, the pain thou hast
love, and thy mer - cy divine; Thou hast drawn me a - way from the
voice gave me com - fort and rest; Let me sing, let me sing, with the
earth I can praise thee no more; Till my soul cloth'd a - new in thy

borne for my sake, Let me sing, let me sing, or my full heart will break.
brink of the grave, And I know of a truth thou art mighty to save.
days gliding by,—O, I wish all the world were as hap-py as I.
like - ness shall wake, Let me sing, let me sing, or my full heart will break.

CHORUS.

Let me sing of the Rock, The firm, a - bid-ing Rock, The

Blessed Rifted Rock of A - ges! Tho' the stormy billows roll, they can

Let me Sing. Concluded.

nev - er reach my soul, I have anchor'd on the Rock of A - ges.

186   Where Shall We Go?

Text.—"To whom shall we go but unto Thee?"

Words by CARRIE M. WILSON.   Music by JNO. R. SWENEY.

1. Where shall we go, when the heart is oppress'd, Where but to Jesus for shelter and rest?
2. Where shall we go, when the tempest is high? Where, but to Jesus, O where can we fly?

Rock'd on the waves of a per-il-ous sea, None can de-liv-er or save us but he.
He is the Life, and that life will he give; Look, and forever with him we may live. *Fine.*

D.S. He, and he only, our wants can relieve: Why are we faithless, O why not believe?

CHORUS.   *D.S.*

Where shall we go, where shall we go? He, and he on - ly our tri - als can know;

3 Where shall we go when the tempter assails?
When o'er our weakness he almost prevails?
Where but to him who was tempted as we?
None can deliver nor save us but he.

4 Where shall we go but to Jesus, our Lord?
He is our refuge; O cling to his Word:
Jesus alone, our Redeemer must be;
None can deliver nor save us but he.

187   Ariel. C. P. M. 8s & 6s.

Words by Chas. Wesley.   Music by Dr. L. Mason.

1. O glo-rious hope of per-fect love! It lifts me up to things above;

It bears on eagles' wings; It gives my rav-ish'd soul a taste,
And makes me for some mo-ments feast

With Je-sus' priests and kings. With Je-sus' priests and kings.

2 Rejoicing now in earnest hope
I stand, and from the mountain top
   See all the land below:
Rivers of milk and honey rise
And all the fruits of paradise
   In endless plenty grow.

3 A land of corn, and wine, and oil,
Favor'd with God's peculiar smile,
   With every blessing blest;

There dwells the Lord our Righteousness,
And keeps his own in perfect peace
   And everlasting rest.

4 O that I might at once go up;
No more on this side Jordan stop,
   But now the land possess;
This moment end my legal years,
Sorrows and sins, and doubts and fears,
   A howling wilderness!

---

188   O LOVE DIVINE, HOW SWEET THOU ART!

1 O love divine, how sweet thou art!
When shall I find my willing heart
   All taken up by thee?
I thirst, I faint, I die to prove
The greatness of Redeeming love,—
   The love of Christ to me.

2 Stronger his love than death or hell;
Its riches are unsearchable;
   The first born sons of light
Desire in vain its depths to see;
They cannot reach the mystery,—
   The length, the breadth, the height.

3 God only knows the love of God;
O that it now were shed abroad
   In this poor stony heart;

For love I sigh, for love I pine;
This only portion, Lord, be mine:
   Be mine this better part.

4 O that I could forever sit
With Mary at the Master's feet!
   Be this my happy choice:
My only care, delight, and bliss,
My joy, my heaven on earth, be this,
   To hear the Bridegroom's voice!

5 O that I could, with favor'd John,
Recline my weary head upon
   The dear Redeemer's breast:
From care, and sin, and sorrow free,
Give me, O Lord, to find in thee
   My everlasting rest.

The World of Light.

Words and Music by O. Snow.

1. There is a beau - ti - ful world, Where saints and an - gels sing;
2. There is a beau - ti - ful world, Where sor-row nev - er comes;

A world where peace and pleasure reigns, And heav'nly prais - es ring.
A world where tears shall nev - er fall In sigh-ing for our home.

CHORUS.

We'll be there, we'll be there: Palms of vict'ry, Crowns of glo - ry we shall wear

Ritard.

In that beau-ti-ful world on high.

3 There is a beautiful world,
  Unseen to mortal sight,
  And darkness never enters there;
  That home is fair and bright.

4 There is a beautiful world
  Of harmony and love;
  O, may we safely enter there,
  And dwell with God above.

190
WORK, FOR THE NIGHT IS COMING.

1 Work, for the night is coming,
  Work through the morning hours;
  Work, while the dew is sparkling,
  Work 'mid springing flowers:
  Work, when the day grows brighter,
  Work in the glowing sun;
  Work, for the night is coming,
  When man's work is done.

2 Work, for the night is coming,
  Work through the sunny noon:
  Fill brightest hours with labor,
  Rest comes sure and soon.

Give every flying minute
  Something to keep in store:
  Work, for the night is coming,
  When man works no more.

3 Work, for the night is coming,
  Under the sunset skies;
  While their bright tints are glowing,
  Work, for daylight flies.
  Work till the last beam fadeth,
  Fadeth to shine no more:
  Work while the night is darkening,
  When man's work is o'er.

SIDNEY DYER.

191 Royal Way of the Cross.

By per. of PHILIP PHILLIPS.   Music by Rev. L. HARTSOUGH.

Fine.

1. { We may spread our couch with ro-ses, And sleep thro' the sum-mer day; }
   { But the soul that in sloth re - pos - es, Is not in the nar - row way. }

D. C. For the roy - al way to heav-en Is the roy - al way of the cross.

If we fol - low the chart that is giv - en, We need not be at a loss,

2 To one who is fond of splendor,
The cross is a heavy load;
And the feet that are soft and tender
Complain of the thorny road:
But the chains of the soul must be riven,
And gold must be as dross;
For the royal way to heaven
Is the royal way of the cross.

3 We say we will walk to-morrow
The path we refuse to-day;
And still, with our lukewarm sorrow,
We shrink from the narrow way:
But in vain we have hoped and striven,
Our gains have proved but loss;
For the royal way to heaven
Is the Royal way of the cross.

192 Rock of Ages.

DR. HASTINGS.

1 Rock of Ages, cleft for me,
Let me hide myself in thee;
Let the water and the blood,
From thy wounded side which flow'd,
Be of sin a double cure,
Save from wrath and make me pure.

2 Could my tears forever flow,
Could my zeal no languor know,
These for sin could not atone;

Thou must save, and thou alone.
In my hand no price I bring,
Simply to thy cross I cling.

3 While I draw this fleeting breath,
When my eyes shall close in death,
When I rise to worlds unknown,
And behold thee on thy throne,
Rock of Ages, cleft for me,
Let me hide myself in thee.

193 FATHER, SON, AND HOLY GHOST.

1 Father, Son, and Holy Ghost,
One in three, and three in one,
As by the celestial host,
Let thy will on earth be done.
Praise by all to thee be given,
Gracious Lord of earth and heav'n!

2 If so poor a worm as I,
May to thy great glory live,
All my actions sanctify,
All my words and thoughts receive;
Claim me for thy service, claim
All I have, and all I am.

3 Take my soul and body's pow'rs;
Take my mem'ry, mind, and will;
All my goods, and all my hours,
All I know, and all I feel;
All I think, or speak, or do:
Take my heart, but make it new!

4 Now, my God, thine own I am;
Now I give thee back thine own:
Freedom, friends, and health and fame,
Consecrate to thee alone.
Thine I live, thrice happy I!
Happier still if thine I die.

194   Jesus, my All!

Words by Rev. G. D. WATSON, D. D.   Music by WM. J. KIRKPATRICK.

1. My heart sings a song From morning till night; A song full of lib - er - ty,
Love, and of light: A song of the Canaan-land, Happy and bright, And
all of my *song* is Jesus.

REFRAIN.

Jesus, Jesus, All of my song is Jesus:

2. All of my rest
3. All of my gift
4. All of my light

From morning till night I sing with de-light,—Jesus, my precious Jesus!

2 My heart hath a rest
    From sin and from fear;
A rest from all doubting,
    Disappointment and care:
A rest like the sky,
    Bending calm o'er the year,—
And all of my *rest* is Jesus.

3 My heart hath a gift,
    With value untold;
A gift of unbounded peace,
    Richer than gold:
A gift that the universe
    Cannot all hold,—
And all of my *gift* is Jesus.

4 My heart hath a light
    In the cloudiest day;
A light which illumines
    Each moment my way:

A light which will not let
    The little one stray,—
And all of my *light* is Jesus.

5 My heart hath a Friend,
    All compassion and love,
Whose speech falls as soft
    As the star-light above:
A friend that abideth,
    And will not remove,—
And that dearest *friend* is Jesus.

6 My heart hath a home,
    And it wanders no more;
A home like to that
    On the glorified shore:
A home where all goodness
    Unbosoms its store,—
And all of my *home* is Jesus.

Let Me Die.

WM. J. KIRKPATRICK.

Fine.

1. O God, my heart doth long for thee, Let me die, Let me die.
Now set my soul at lib - er - ty, Let me die, Let me die.

D.C. My Sav - iour calls, I'm go - ing forth, Let me die, Let me die.

D.C.

To all the tri-fling things of earth, They're now to me of lit - tle worth:

2 Thy slaying power in me display,
Let me die, let me die.
I must be dead from day to day,
Let me die, let me die.
Unto the world and its applause,
To all the customs, fashions, laws,
Of those who hate the humbling cross,
Let me die, let me die.

3 My friends may say, "I'll ruined be,"
Let me die, let me die.
But all I leave, and follow thee,
Let me die, let me die.
Their arguments will never weigh,
Nor stand the trying judgment day;
Help me to cast them all away,
Let me die, let me die.

4 Oh, I must die to scoffs and jeers,
Let me die, let me die.
I must be freed from slavish fears,
Let me die, let me die.
So dead that no desire shall rise
To pass for good, or great, or wise,
In any but my Saviour's eyes!
Let me die, let me die.

5 If Christ would live and reign in me,
I must die, I must die;
Like him I crucified must be,
I must die, I must die.
Lord, drive the nails, nor heed the groans,
My flesh may writhe and make its moans,
But in this way and this alone,
I must die, I must die.

6 Begin at once to drive the nails,
Let me die, let me die:
Oh, suffer not my heart to fail,
Let me die, let me die.
Jesus, I look to thee for power
To help me to endure the hour
When, crucified by sovereign power,
I shall die, I shall die.

7 When I am dead, then, Lord, to thee,
I shall live, I shall live;
My time, my strength, my all to thee,
Will I give, will I give.
Oh, may the Son now make me free!
Here, Lord, I give my all to thee,
For time and for eternity
I will live, I will live.

196

Come to Jesus.

1. Come to Je-sus, come to Je-sus, Come to Je-sus just now: Just now come

to Jesus, Come to Jesus just now.

2 He will save you just now, &c.
3 O believe him just now, &c.
4 He is able.
5 He is willing.
6 He'll receive you.
7 He will hear you.
8 He'll forgive you.
9 He will cleanse you.
10 Jesus loves you.
11 Only trust him.

What's the News?

Fine.

1. Where'er we meet, you al-ways say, What's the news? What's the news?
Pray, what's the or-der of the day? What's the news? What's the news?

D.C. And triumph'd o - ver death and hell: That's the news! That's the news!

D.C.

Oh, I have got good news to tell, My Saviour hath done all things well,

2 His work's reviving all around;
　That's the news! that's the news!
His saints are making songs resound;
　That's the news! that's the news!
Poor sinners, doomed in sin and woe,
Are now rejoicing as they go,
And shouting glory here below:
　That's the news! that's the news!

3 He took my sorrows all away;
　That's the news! that's the news!
He turned my darkness into day;
　That's the news! that's the news!
Yes, Jesus saves me now, I know,
His blood has wash'd me white as snow,
And now I'm glad his love to show:
　That's the news! that's the news!

4 And Christ, the Lord, can save you now,
　That's the news! that's the news!
Your sinful heart he can renew;
　That's the news! that's the news!
This moment, if for sins you grieve,
This moment, if you now believe,
A full acquittal you'll receive:
　That's the news! that's the news!

5 And now if any one should say,—
　What's the news? what's the news?
Oh, tell them you've begun to pray;
　That's the news! that's the news!
That you have join'd the conqu'ring band,
And now with joy, at God's command,
You're marching to the better land:
　That's the news! that's the news!

---

198 O, WHO'LL STAND UP FOR JESUS?
(No. 13 in " BEULAH SONGS.")

1 O, who'll stand up for Jesus,
　The lowly Nazarene?
And raise the blood-stain'd banner
　Amid the hosts of sin?

Chorus.
The Cross for Christ I'll cherish,
　Its crucifixion bear;
All hail! reproach or sorrow,
　If Jesus leads me there.

2 O, who will follow Jesus,
　Amid reproach and shame?
Where others shrink or falter,
　Who'll glory in his name?

3 Though fierce may rage the battle,
　And wild the storm may blow,—
Though friends may go forever,
　Who will with Jesus go?

4 My all to Christ I've given,
　My talents, time and voice,
Myself, my reputation,
　The lone way is my choice.

5 O, Jesus, Jesus, Jesus,
　My all-sufficient Friend!
Come, fold me to thy bosom,
　E'en to the journey's end.

REV. L. HARTSOUGH.

199 Happy in the Love of Jesus.

Words by HENRIETTA E. BLAIR.   Music by WM. J. KIRKPATRICK.

1. Bright is the day-star shining for me, Happy in the love of Je - sus;
2. He has redeem'd me, I am his own, Happy in the love of Je - sus;
3. How I am honor'd, how I am blest, Happy in the love of Je - sus;
4. Firm is my anchor, steadfast and sure, Happy in the love of Je - sus;

Now from my bondage grace makes me free, Happy in the love of Je - sus.
Drawn by his mer-cy near to his throne, Happy in the love of Je - sus.
Un - der his ban-ner sweet-ly I rest, Happy in the love of Je - sus.
All things with pa-tience I can en-dure, Happy in the love of Je - sus.

CHORUS.

Praise from my full heart loudly shall ring, Born of the Spirit, child of a King;

Heir to his glo - ry, now will I sing,—Happy in the love of Je - sus.

I Love Thee. 11s.

Arr. by W. J. K.

1. I love thee, I love thee, I love thee, my Lord; I love thee, my Saviour, I

D.S. But how much I love thee, I

Fine.

love thee, my God; I love thee, I love thee, and that thou dost know:

nev-er can show.

D.S.

2 I'm happy, I'm happy, O wondrous account!
My joys are immortal; I stand on the mount!
I gaze on my treasure, and long to be there
With Jesus and angels, my kindred so dear.

3 O Jesus, my Saviour! with thee I am blest!
My life and salvation, my joy and my rest!
Thy name be my theme, and thy love be my song,
Thy grace shall inspire both my heart and my tongue.

4 O, who's like my Saviour! He's Salem's bright King!
He smiles, and he loves me, and learns me to sing:
I'll praise him, I'll praise him, with notes loud and shrill,
While rivers of pleasure my spirit doth fill.

---

201   WHAT A FRIEND WE HAVE IN JESUS.

(No. 121 in "BEULAH SONGS.")

1 What a Friend we have in Jesus,
All our sins and griefs to bear;
What a privilege to carry
Everything to God in prayer.
Oh, what peace we often forfeit,
Oh, what needless pain we bear—
All because we do not carry
Everything to God in prayer.

2 Have we trials and temptations?
Is there trouble anywhere?
We should never be discouraged:
Take it to the Lord in prayer.

Can we find a Friend so faithful,
Who will all our sorrows share?
Jesus knows our every weakness,
Take it to the Lord in prayer.

3 Are we weak and heavy-laden,
Cumbered with a load of care?
Precious Saviour, still our Refuge,—
Take it to the Lord in prayer.
Do thy friends despise, forsake thee?
Take it to the Lord in prayer:
In his arms he'll take and shield thee,
Thou wilt find a solace there.

HORATIUS BONAR, D. D.

Come to Jesus.

By Permission.

Words and Music by Rev. J. H. STOCKTON.

1. Come, ev-'ry soul by sin oppress'd, There's mer-cy with the Lord;
And he will sure-ly give you rest, By trust-ing in his Word.

CHORUS.

Come to Je-sus, Come to Je-sus, Come to Je-sus now!

He will save you, He will save you, He will save you now.

2 For Jesus shed his precious blood,
　Rich blessings to bestow;
Plunge now into the crimson flood
　That washes white as snow.

3 Yes, Jesus is the truth, the way,
　That leads you into rest;
Believe in him, without delay,
　And you are fully blest.

4 O Jesus, blessed Jesus, dear,
　I'm coming now to thee;
Since thou hast made the way so clear,
　And full salvation free.

5 Come, then, and join this holy band,
　And on to glory go;
To dwell in that celestial land
　Where joys immortal flow.

203　COME, HUMBLE SINNER, IN WHOSE BREAST.

1 Come, humble sinner, in whose breast
　A thousand thoughts revolve,
Come, with your guilt and fear oppress'd,
　And make this last resolve:—

2 I'll go to Jesus, though my sin
　Like mountains round me close;
I know his courts, I'll enter in,
　Whatever may oppose.

3 Prostrate I'll lie before his throne,
　And there my guilt confess;

I'll tell him I'm a wretch undone,
　Without his sovereign grace.

4 Perhaps he will admit my plea,
　Perhaps will hear my prayer;
But, if I perish, I will pray,
　And perish only there.

5 I can but perish, if I go;
　I am resolv'd to try:
For if I stay away, I know
　I must forever die.　EDMUND JONES.

Bridgewater. L. M.

1. I thirst, thou wounded Lamb of God, To wash me in thy cleansing blood; To dwell with-in thy wounds: then pain To dwell with-in thy wounds: then pain Is sweet, and life or death is gain.

To dwell within thy wounds: then pain To dwell within thy wounds: then pain Is sweet, and life or death is gain.

2 Take my poor heart, and let it be
Forever closed to all but thee;
Seal thou my breast, and let me wear
That pledge of love forever there.

3 How blest are they who still abide
Close sheltered in thy bleeding side!

Who thence their life and strength derive,
And by thee move, and in thee live.

4 What are our works but sin and death,
Till thou thy quickening Spirit breathe?
Thou giv'st the power thy grace to move;
O wondrous grace! O boundless love!

205

COME, SINNERS, TO THE GOSPEL FEAST.

1 Come, sinners, to the gospel feast;
Let every soul be Jesus' guest:
Ye need not one be left behind,
For God hath bidden all mankind.

2 Sent by my Lord, on you I call;
The invitation is to all: —
Come all the world! come, sinner, thou!
All things in Christ are ready now.

3 Come, all ye souls by sin oppressed,
Ye restless wand'rers after rest;

Ye poor, and maimed, and halt, and blind,
In Christ a hearty welcome find.

4 My message as from God receive;
Ye all may come to Christ and live:
O let his love your hearts constrain,
Nor suffer him to die in vain.

5 See him set forth before your eyes
That precious, bleeding sacrifice!
His offer'd benefits embrace,
And freely now be sav'd by grace.

Speak for Jesus.

Words by SALLIE M. SMITH. Music by JNO. R. SWENEY.

1. Come, let us tell what the Lord for us hath done, Of the tri-als and the
2. Come, let us tell of the many answer'd prayers That so oft have fill'd our
3. Come, let us tell what the Lord is do-ing still: Do we find a constant

toils he has bro't us safely thro'; Of the bat-tles we have fought, and the
hearts with a grateful song of love, When in sim-ple trusting faith we have
peace in his ser-vice day by day? Are we bending ev-'ry pow'r in sub-

vict'ry's we have won, Thro' the grace that he bestows on the faithful and the true.
cast on him our cares, And the spirit from his throne has descended like a dove.
mis-sion to his will? Let us cheer each other on while we journey by the way.

CHORUS.

Trusting in the mer-its of an all a-ton-ing Saviour, Trusting in the promise of a soul-a-bid-ing rest; Lean-ing on the mer-cy that so

graciously has led us, How can we be si-lent, with its fullness ev-er blest?

---

207 Chapin. S. M.

Words by JAMES MONTGOMERY.

Music by JOSHUA GILL.

1. O where shall rest be found, Rest for the wea - ry soul?

'Twere vain the o - cean's depths to sound, Or pierce to cith - er pole.

2 The world can never give
  The bliss for which we sigh;
  'Tis not the whole of life to live,
  Nor all of death to die.

3 Beyond this vale of tears
  There is a life above,
  Unmeasured by the flight of years,
  And all that life is love.

4 There is a death, whose pang
  Outlasts the fleeting breath:
  O what eternal horrors hang
  Around the second death!

5 Thou God of truth and grace,
  Teach us that death to shun;
  Lest we be banished from thy face,
  Forevermore undone.

208 He Saves me through and through.

Words by FANNY J. CROSBY.   Music by JNO. R. SWENEY.

1. The blood that Je-sus shed for me When groaning, dy-ing on the tree,
2. In per-fect trust I now re-sign My all to him whose will is mine;
3. No angel tongue such praise can bring, Nor learn the song that now I sing
4. I know not what my joy will be, When face to face my Lord I see,

From all transgression cleanseth me, And saves me through and through.
He fills my soul with love divine, And saves me through and through.
To him, my Prophet, Priest and King, Who saves me through and through.
But this I know, he cleanseth me, And saves me through and through.

CHORUS.

Sav'd, sav'd, yes, I am sav'd, My heart is cre-a-ted a-new;

The blood of Je-sus cleanseth me, And saves me through and through.

Jesus for Me.

W. J. K.

WM. J. KIRKPATRICK.

1. Je - sus, my Saviour, is all things to me, O, what a Won-der-ful
2. Je - sus in sickness, and Je - sus in health, Je - sus in pov - er - ty,
3. He is my Ref-uge, my Rock and my Tow'r, He is my Fortress, my
4. He is my Prophet, my Priest and my King, He is my Bread of Life,
5. Je - sus in sor-row, in joy, or in pain, Je - sus my Treasure in

Sav - iour is He: Guid-ing, pro-tect-ing, o'er life's roll-ing sea,
com - fort or wealth, Sunshine or tem-pest, what-ev - er it be,
Strength and my pow'r; Life Ev - er - last-ing, my Day'sman is He,
Fount-ain and Spring; Bright Sun of Righteousness, Day-star is He,
loss or in gain; Constant Com-pan-ion, where'er I may be,

CHORUS.

Might - y De - liv - 'rer— Je - sus for me. Je - sus for me,
He is my safe-ty:— Je - sus for me.
Bless - ed Re - deem-er— Je - sus for me.
Horn of Sal - va - tion— Je - sus for me.
Liv - ing or dy - ing— Je - sus for me!

Je - sus for me, All the time, ev - 'ry-where, Je - sus for me.

Windham. L. M.

1. Show pity, Lord, O Lord, for-give; Let a re-pent-ing reb-el live:
2. My crimes are great, but don't sur-pass The pow'r and glory of thy grace;

Are not thy mercies large and free? May not a sin-ner trust in thee?
Great God, thy nature hath no bound, So let thy pard'ning love be found.

3
O wash my soul from every sin,
And make my guilty conscience clean;
Here on my heart the burden lies,
And past offences pain my eyes.

4
My lips with shame my sins confess,
Against thy law, against thy grace;
Lord, should thy judgments grow severe,
I am condemn'd, but thou art clear.

5
Should sudden vengeance seize my breath,
I must pronounce thee just, in death;
And if my soul were sent to hell,
Thy righteous law approves it well.

6
Yet save a trembling sinner, Lord,
Whose hope, still hov'ring round thy word,
Would light on some sweet promise there, —
Some sure support against despair.

211

WHILE LIFE PROLONG ITS PRECIOUS LIGHT.

1
While life prolongs its precious light,
  Mercy is found, and peace is given;
But soon, ah, soon, approaching night
  Shall blot out every hope of heaven.

2
While God invites, how blest the day!
  How sweet the Gospel's charming sound!
Come, sinners, haste, O haste away,
  While yet a pard'ning God is found.

3
Soon, borne on time's most rapid wing,
  Shall death command you to the grave, —

Before his bar your spirits bring,
  And none be found to hear or save.

4
In that lone land of deep despair,
  No Sabbath's heavenly light shall rise, —
No God regard your bitter prayer,
  No Saviour call you to the skies.

5
Now God invites: how blest the day!
  How sweet the Gospel's charming sound!
Come, sinners, haste, O haste away,
  While yet a pard'ning God is found.

The Child of a King.

(As Sung by Mrs. M. J. Inskip.)

Words by HATTIE E. BUELL.   Arr. from a Melody by Rev. JOHN B. SUMNER.

1. My Fa-ther is rich in houses and lands, He holdeth the wealth of the
2. My Father's own Son, the Saviour of men, Once wander'd o'er earth as the
3. I once was an out-cast stranger on earth, A sin-ner by choice, an
4. A tent or a cot-tage, why should I care? They're building a palace for

world in his hands! Of rubies and diamonds, of sil-ver and gold, His
poor-est of men; But now he is reigning for-ev-er on high, And will
al - ien by birth! But I've been a-dopt-ed, my name's written down,—An
me o - ver there! Tho' exiled from home, yet still I may sing: All

CHORUS.

cof - fers are full,—he has rich-es un-told. I'm the child of a King, The
give me a home in heav'n by and by.
heir to a man-sion, a robe, and a crown.
glo - ry to God, I'm the child of a King!

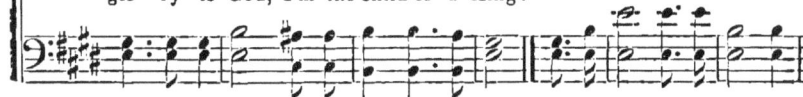

ad lib.

child of a King! With Je - sus, my Saviour, I'm the child of a King!

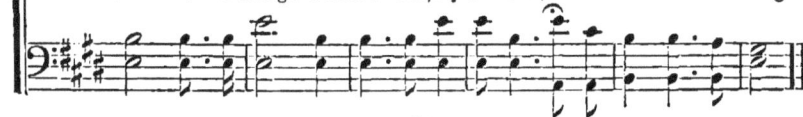

Sanctification.   C. M.

Arr. from S. HUBBARD.

1. For - ev - er here my rest shall be, Close to thy bleed-ing side;
2. My dy-ing Sav-iour and my God, Fountain for guilt and sin,

This all my hope, and all my plea, For me the Sav-iour died.
Sprin-kle me ev - er with thy blood, And cleanse and keep me clean.

3 Wash me, and make me thus thine own;
    Wash me, and mine thou art;
Wash me, but not my feet alone,—
    My hands, my head, my heart.

4 Th'atonement of thy blood apply,
    Till faith to sight improve;
Till hope in full fruition die,
    And all my soul be love.

---

214   I SAW A WAY-WORN TRAVELLER.
(No. 12 in "BEULAH SONGS.")

1 I saw a way-worn trav'ler
    In tatter'd garments clad;
And, struggling up the mountain,
    It seem'd that he was sad:
His back was laden heavy,
    His strength was almost gone;
Yet he shouted, as he journeyed,
    Deliverance will come.

Cho.—Then palms of victory,
    Crowns of glory,
    Palms of victory
    I shall bear.

2 The summer sun was shining,
    The sweat was on his brow,
His garments worn and dusty,
    His step seemed very slow:
But he kept pressing onward,
    For he was wending home,
Still shouting, as he journeyed,
    Deliverance will come.

3 The songsters in the arbor,
    That grew beside the way,
Attracted his attention,
    Inviting his delay:
His watchword being "Onward,"
    He stopped his ears and ran,

Still shouting, as he journeyed,
    Deliverance will come.

4 I saw him in the evening,
    The sun was bending low,
Had overtopped the mountain,
    And reached the vale below:
He saw the golden city,
    His everlasting home,
And shouted loud hosanna!
    Deliverance will come.

5 While gazing on that city,
    Just o'er the narrow flood,
A band of holy angels
    Came from the throne of God:
They bore him on their pinions
    Safe o'er the dashing foam,
And joined him in his triumph,—
    Deliverance has come.

6 I heard the song of triumph
    They sang upon that shore,
Saying, "Jesus has redeemed us,
    To suffer nevermore!"
Then casting his eyes backward,
    On the race which he had ran,
He shouted loud hosanna!
    Deliverance has come.

215 Light for Me.

Words by G. W. STORY.   Music by JNO. R. SWENEY.

1. A light is shining now for me, With radiant lus-tre beaming;
2. That light that shin-eth now for me, With fadeless beau-ty glowing,
3. That light re-splen-dent from the tomb Shone out the earth a - dorn-ing,
4. O light, whose brightness in my soul Proclaims redemption's sto - ry,

A light that ev - 'ry eye may see From Calvary's mountain streaming.
Still guides the lost to yon-der fount For ev - 'ry crea-ture flow-ing.
When Je-sus, rising, conquer'd death, And an-gels hail'd the morn-ing.
'Twill lead me on with steady ray, And be my song in glo - ry!

CHORUS.

O love e - ter - nal, can it be, My Saviour gave his life for me?

For me, for me, — He gave his life for me!
For me, for me,

216   It Reaches Me.

Words by MARY D. JAMES.   Music by JNO. R. SWENEY.

1. Oh, this ut - ter-most sal-va-tion! 'Tis a fount-ain full and free,
2. How a-maz-ing God's compassion, That so vile a worm should prove
3. Je - sus, Saviour, I a - dore thee! Now thy love I will pro-claim;

Pure, ex-haust-less, ev - er flow-ing, Wondrous grace! it reach-es me!
This stu-pend-ous bliss of heav-en, This unmeasured wealth of love!
I will tell the bless-ed sto-ry, I will mag-ni-fy thy name!

CHORUS.

It reaches me! it reach-es me! Wondrous grace! it reach-es me!

Pure, ex-haust-less, ev - er flowing, Wondrous grace! it reach-es me!

From "THE GARNER," by per of JNO. J. HOOD.

217   SWEET HOUR OF PRAYER.

1

Sweet hour of prayer, sweet hour of prayer,
That calls me from a world of care,
And bids me, at my Father's throne,
Make all my wants and wishes known!
In seasons of distress and grief,
My soul has often found relief,
And oft escaped the tempter's snare,
By thy return, sweet hour of prayer.

2

Sweet hour of prayer, sweet hour of prayer,
Thy wings shall my petition bear
To him, whose truth and faithfulness
Engage the waiting soul to bless:
And since he bids me seek his face,
Believe his word, and trust his grace,
I'll cast on him my every care,
And wait for thee, sweet hour of prayer.

3

Sweet hour of prayer, sweet hour of prayer,
May I thy consolation share,
Till, from Mount Pisgah's lofty height,
I view my home, and take my flight:
This robe of flesh I'll drop, and rise
To seize the everlasting prize;
And shout, while passing through the air,
Farewell, farewell, sweet hour of prayer!

WILLIAM W. WALFORD.

218   I'm Kneeling at the Cross.

Words by Rev. J. PARKER. By per.   Music by S. J. VAIL.

1. The blood, the blood is all my plea, Nor should a sin-ner won-der,
2. I rest, I rest supremely blest, With-out a care to can-ker;
3. My cup, my cup it run-neth o'er, With joy ce-les-tial brimming;
4. The blood, the blood is all my song, I have no bliss without it;

For guil-ty stain and stinging pain Hath tore my heart a-sun-der!
No gloom-y night, my path is bright, My hope holds like an an-chor.
On wings of love I soar a-bove, His hal-le-lu-jahs hymning.
From ev-'ry stain it makes me clean, My life and lip shall shout it.

CHORUS.

But now I'm kneeling at the cross, Washing in the crimson tide,

And cleans'd, I tar-ry at the fountain Open'd at my Saviour's side.

175

219 I left it all with Jesus.

Words and Music adapted and arranged by W. J. K.

1. O, I left it all with Je-sus, long a-go, long a-go, My

D.C. From my wea-ry heart the bur-den roll'd a-way, roll'd a-way, And

Fine.

sin-ful-ness I brought him and my woe; And when by faith I

now I'm sing-ing glo-ry, hap-py day.

D.C.

saw him on the tree, And heard his still small whisper, "'Tis for thee,"

2
O, I leave it all with Jesus, for he knows
Just how to take the bitter from life's woes,
And how to gild the tear-drop with his smile,
To make the desert garden bloom awhile;
Then, with all my weakness, leaning on his
  might,
My soul sings hallelujah, all is light.

3
O, I leave it all with Jesus, day by day,
My faith can firmly trust him, come what
  may, [rest,
For hope has dropp'd her anchor, found her
Within the calm sure haven of his breast:
And oh! 'tis joy of heaven to abide
Close to my dear Redeemer, at his side.

From "Songs of Triumph," by per.

220   Coronation. C. M.   Oliver Holden.

1 All hail the pow'r of Jesus' name!
   Let angels prostrate fall;
 Bring forth the royal diadem,
   And crown him Lord of all!

2 Ye chosen seed of Israel's race,
   Ye ransom'd from the fall,
 Hail him who saves you by his grace,
   And crown him Lord of all!

3 Sinners, whose love can ne'er forget
   The wormwood and the gall,

Go, spread your trophies at his feet,
   And crown him Lord of all!

4 Let every kindred, every tribe,
   On this terrestrial ball,
 To him all majesty ascribe,
   And crown him Lord of all!

5 O that with yonder sacred throng
   We at his feet may fall;
 We'll join the everlasting song,
   And crown him Lord of all!

221   "Lost in Sight of Home." *

H. L. G.   Dr. H. L. Gilmour.

1. Lost in sight of home, where lov'd ones Watch the wea-ry hours in vain,
2. Lost in sight of home, where moth-er Fond-ly gaz'd up-on her boy,
3. Lost in sight of home, where Fa-ther Waits to meet his wayward child;
4. Lost in sight of home, where brother's Last good-by still lin-gers dear,
5. Lost to many a friend and lov'd one, Watching now in heaven's bright dome;

Long-ing for fa-mil-iar foot-steps That seem not to come a-gain.
While with upturn'd eyes he'd rev-el In her glee-ful songs of joy.
Longs to wel-come back and par-don, Longs to see him re-con-cil'd.
And that sis-ter's kiss at part-ing Brings to mind the fall-ing tear.
Lost while Je-sus waits to wel-come, Lost, and lost in sight of home.

CHORUS.

Haste, O haste a Saviour's call-ing, Through the darken'd mist of sin;

See, the Gos-pel light still flash-es And in-vites the wand'rer in.

* During one of the severe storms that visited Colorado, a young man perished in sight of home. In his bewilderment he passed and repassed his own cottage to lie down and die almost in range with the "light in the window" which his young wife had placed there to guide him home. All alone she watched the long night through, listening in vain for the footsteps that would come no more; for long before the morning dawned the icy touch of death had forever stilled that warm, loving heart. The sad death was made still sadder by the fact that he was lost in sight of home.

How many wanderers from the Father's house are lost in sight of home, in the full glare of the Gospel light! They have the open Bible, overflowing with its calls and promises, the faithful warnings from the sacred desk, the manifestations of God's providence, all tending to direct their footsteps heavenward; and yet from all these they turn away, waiting for the more convenient season, and are lost, at last, in sight of the many mansions.—"Forward."

Litany Hymn. 7s. Double.

Fine.

1. Je - sus, plant and root in me   All the mind that was in thee; }
Set - tled peace I then shall find; Je - sus' is   a   qui-et mind. }

D.S. Meek-ly   on   my God re - clin'd, Je - sus' is   a   gen-tle mind.

D.C.

2. An - ger I   no more shall feel, —Al-ways   e - ven, al - ways still;

3 I shall suffer and fulfil
   All my Father's gracious will;
   Be in all alike resign'd;
   Jesus' is a patient mind.

4 When 'tis deeply rooted here,
   Perfect love shall cast out fear;
   Fear doth servile spirits bind;
   Jesus' is a noble mind.

5 I shall nothing know beside
   Jesus, and him crucified;
   Perfectly to him be join'd;
   Jesus' is a loving mind.

6 I shall triumph evermore;
   Gratefully my God adore;
   God so good, so true, so kind;
   Jesus' is a thankful mind.

7 Lowly, loving, meek and pure,
   I shall to the end endure;
   Be no more to sin inclined:
   Jesus' is a constant mind.

8 I shall fully be restored
   To the image of my Lord;
   Witnessing to all mankind,
   Jesus' is a perfect mind.

SAVIOUR OF THE SIN-SICK SOUL.
(SECOND HYMN.)

1 Saviour of the sin-sick soul,
   Give me faith to make me whole;
   Finish thy great work of grace;
   Cut it short in righteousness.
   Speak the second time,—Be clean!
   Take away my inbred sin;
   Every stumbling-block remove;
   Cast it out by perfect love.

2 Nothing less will I require;
   Nothing more can I desire:
   None but Christ to me be given;
   None but Christ in earth or heaven.
   O that I might now decrease!
   O that all I am might cease!
   Let me into nothing fall;
   Let my Lord be all in all.

223

ARISE, MY SOUL, ARISE.

1 Arise, my soul, arise;
   Shake off thy guilty fears:
   The bleeding Sacrifice
   In my behalf appears:
   Before the throne my Surety stands,
   My name is written on his hands.
2 He ever lives above,
   For me to intercede;
   His all-redeeming love,
   His precious blood to plead;
   His blood atoned for all our race,
   And sprinkles now the throne of grace.
3 Five bleeding wounds he bears,
   Received on Calvary;
   They pour effectual prayers,

   They strongly plead for me:
   Forgive him, O forgive! they cry,
   Nor let that ransom'd sinner die.
4 The Father hears him pray,
   His dear anointed One;
   He cannot turn away
   The presence of his Son;
   His Spirit answers to the blood,
   And tells me I am born of God.
5 My God is reconciled;
   His pard'ning voice I hear;
   He owns me for his child;
   I can no longer fear;
   With confidence I now draw nigh,
   And Father, Abba, Father, cry.

224 We have an Anchor.

PRISCILLA J. OWENS. Music by WM. J. KIRKPATRICK. By per.

1. Will your an-chor hold in the storms of life, When the clouds unfold their
2. It is safely moor'd, 'twill the storm withstand, For 'tis well secur'd by the
3. It will firm-ly hold in the straits of fear, When the breakers have told the
4. It will sure-ly hold in the floods of death, When the waters cold chill our
5. When our eyes be-hold thro' the gath'ring night The cit-y of gold, our

wings of strife? When the strong tides lift, and the ca-bles strain, Will your
Saviour's hand; And the ca-bles, pass'd from his heart to mine, Can de-
reef is near, Tho' the tempest rave and the wild winds blow, Not an
lat-est breath, On the ris-ing tide it can nev-er fail, While our
har-bor bright, We shall an-chor fast by the heav'nly shore, With the

REFRAIN.

an-chor drift, or firm re-main? We have an anchor that keeps the soul
fy the blast, thro' strength di-vine.
angry wave shall our bark o'erflow.
hopes a-bide with-in the veil.
storms all past for-ev-er-more.

steadfast and sure while the billows roll, Fasten'd to the Rock which

can-not move, Grounded firm and deep In the Sav-iour's love.

225   In the Secret of His Presence.

Words by Rev. HENRY BURTON, M. A.   Music by JNO. R. SWENEY.

Moderato.

1. In the se-cret of his presence, I am kept from strife of tongues;
2. In the se-cret of his presence, All the darkness dis-ap-pears;
3. In the se-cret of his presence, Nev-er-more can foes a-larm;
4. In the se-cret of his presence, Is a sweet, un-broken rest:

His pa-vil-ion is a-round me, And with-in are ceaseless songs!
For a sun, that knows no setting, Throws a rain-bow on my tears.
In the shadow of the Highest, I can meet them with a psalm:
Pleasures, joys, in glorious full-ness, Making earth like E-den blest:

Stormy winds his word ful-fil-ing, Beat with-out, but can-not harm,
So the day grows ev-er light-er, Broad'ning to the per-fect noon;
For the strong pa-vil-ion hides me, Turns their fi-'ry darts a-side,
So my peace grows deep and deeper, Widening as it nears the sea,

For the Master's voice is still-ing Storm and tempest to a calm.
So the day grows ev-er brighter, Heav'n is coming, near and soon.
And I know, whate'er be-tides me, I shall live be-cause he died!
For my Saviour is my Keeper, Keeping mine, and keeping me!

In the Secret of His Presence. Concluded.

CHORUS.

In the se — — — cret of his presence, Je-sus keeps,......
In the se-cret of his presence, Je - sus

.... I know not how; In the shadow of the
keeps, I know not how; I know not how:

— — — ow of the high - est,
highest, In the shadow of the Highest, I am rest-ing, hid - ing now.

226

(No. 21 in "BEULAH SONGS.")

I HEAR THY WELCOME VOICE.

1 I hear thy welcome voice,
  That calls me, Lord, to thee,
For cleansing in thy precious blood
  That flowed on Calvary.

  Chorus.
I am coming, Lord!
  Coming now to thee!
Wash me, cleanse me in the blood
  That flowed on Calvary.

2 Though coming weak and vile,
  Thou dost my strength assure;
Thou dost my vileness fully cleanse,
  Till spotless all, and pure.

3 'Tis Jesus calls me on
  To Perfect Faith and Love.

To Perfect Hope, and Peace, and Trust,
  For Earth and Heaven above.

4 'Tis Jesus who confirms
  The blessed work within,
By adding grace to welcomed grace,
  Where reigned the power of sin.

5 And he the witness gives
  To loyal hearts and free,
That every promise is fulfilled,
  If faith but brings the plea.

6 All hail! atoning blood!
  All hail! redeeming grace!
All hail! the gift of Christ, our Lord,
  Our strength and righteousness.

Rev. L. HARTSOUGH.

"I have written unto you, young men, because ye are strong, and the word of God abideth in you, and ye have overcome the wicked one."—1 John, 2: 14.
"And they overcame him by the blood of the Lamb."—Rev. 12: 11.

WM. J. KIRKPATRICK.

QUESTION.

1 John, 5: 5, 4.	1. Who, who is he?	Who, who is he?	Who, who is he that
Rev. 3: 5.	2. What shall he wear?	What shall he wear?	What shall he wear that
Rev. 2: 7.	3. What shall he eat?	What shall he eat?	What shall he eat that
Rev. 3: 12.	4. What shall he be?	What shall he be?	What shall he be that

RESPONSE.

o - ver - com-eth by the blood of the Lamb?   He that be -
o - ver - com-eth by the blood of the Lamb?   He shall be
o - ver - com-eth by the blood of the Lamb?   He shall
o - ver - com-eth by the blood of the Lamb?   He shall be a

lieveth and is born of God,   He that be - liev-eth and is
clothed in rai - ment white,   He shall be clothed in
eat of the tree of life,   He shall eat of the
pil - lar in the temple of God,   He shall be a pil - lar in the

born of God,   He that be - liev - eth and is
rai - ment white,   He shall be clothed in
tree of life,   He shall eat of the
temple of God,   He shall be a pil - lar in the

born of God, Shall o - ver - come by the blood.
rai - ment white, That o - ver - comes by the blood.
tree of life, That o - ver - comes by the blood.
temple of God, That o - ver - comes by the blood.

CHORUS.

O, the precious, precious blood! O, the cleansing, heal - ing flood!

O, the pow'r and the love of God, Thro' the blood of the Lamb!

5

Rev. 3: 5. ‖: What shall he hear? :‖ that overcometh
By the blood of the Lamb?
‖: He shall hear his name con-|fessed in heaven, :‖
That overcomes by the blood.

6

Rev. 21: 7. ‖: What shall he have? :‖ that overcometh
By the blood of the Lamb?
‖: God will give him all things, and | make him His son, :‖
That overcomes by the blood.

7

Rev. 3: 21. ‖: Where shall he sit? :‖ that overcometh
By the blood of the Lamb?
‖: He shall sit with | Jesus, on His throne, :‖
That overcomes by the blood.

8

1 John, 5: 4. ‖: What is the victory? :‖ that overcometh
By the blood of the Lamb?
‖: Faith is the victory that | overcometh :‖
By the blood of the Lamb.

228 Sing, O Sing the Love of Jesus.

Words by MAY CLIFTON.

Music by WM. J. KIRKPATRICK.

1. Sing, oh sing the love of Je - sus, Boundless, deep unmeasured love;
2. Sing, oh sing the love of Je - sus, Ren-der hearty thanks and praise;
3. An - gel lips will join our an - them, Thro' the sky the sound prolong;
4. Pow'r and might and bliss e - ter - nal Now and ev - er-more shall be

Let the soul - in - spir-ing cho - rus Ring thro' all the courts a - bove.
While he gives us life and be - ing, Praise him on through endless days.
Heav'nly hosts take up the cho - rus, And with rap-ture swell the song.
Un - to him who lov'd and sav'd us With a love so full and free.

CHORUS.

Sing, oh sing............. the love of Je - - - - sus,

the love of Je - sus, Sing, O sing the love of Je - sus,

Heav'n and earth........... re-peat the strain;

re-peat the strain, Heav'n and earth re-peat the strain;

Sing, O sing,........... till ev - 'ry na - - - - tion

till ev - 'ry na - tion, Sing, O sing, till ev - 'ry na - tion

Ech - oes on............ the sweet re - frain.

the sweet re - frain,

Ech - oes on the sweet re - frain.

229

At the Fountain.

Arranged for this Work.

1. Of him who did sal - va - tion bring, I'm at the fountain drink-ing;
2. Ask but his grace, and lo! 'tis giv'n, I'm at the fountain drink-ing;

CHORUS.

I could for-ev-er think and sing, I'm on my journey home. Glo - ry to
Ask, and he turns your hell to heav'n, I'm on my journey home.

God, I'm at the fountain drinking, Glory to God, I'm on my journey home.

last v.—My soul is sat-is-fied.

3 Though sin and sorrow wound my soul,
  I'm at the fountain drinking;
Jesus, thy balm will make it whole,
  I'm on my journey home.

4 Let all the world fall down and know
  I'm at the fountain drinking;
That none but God such love can show,
  I'm on my journey home.

5 Where'er I am, where'er I move,
  I'm at the fountain drinking;
I meet the object of my love,
  I'm on my journey home.

6 Insatiate to this spring I fly,
  I'm at the fountain drinking;
I drink, and yet am ever dry,
  I'm on my journey home.

Sing On.

Words by CARRIE M. WILSON.

Music by JNO. R. SWENEY.

1. Sing on, ye joy - ful pil - grims, Nor think the mo-ments long;
2. Sing on, ye joy - ful pil - grims, While here on earth we stay;
3. Sing on, ye joy - ful pil - grims, The time will not be long

My faith is heav'nward ris - ing With ev - 'ry tune-ful song.
Let songs of home and Je - sus Be - guile each fleet-ing day.
Till in our Fa - ther's king-dom We swell a no - bler song:

Lo! on the mount of bless - ing, The glo - rious mount I stand,
Sing on the grand old sto - ry Of his re - deem-ing love;
Where those we love are wait - ing To greet us on the shore,

And look - ing o - ver Jor - dan, I see the promis'd land!
The ev - er - last-ing cho - rus That fills the realms a - bove.
We'll meet be - yond the riv - er, Where surg - es roll no more,

Sing On. Concluded.

Sing on; O, bliss-ful mu-sic, With ev-'ry note you raise,

My heart is fill'd with rap-ture, My soul is lost in praise.

Sing on; O, bliss-ful mu-sic, With ev-'ry note you raise,
Sing on; bliss-ful, bliss-ful mu-sic,

My heart is fill'd with rap-ture, My soul is lost in praise.

231 To Seek and Save.

Text—"*The Son of Man has come to seek and to save that which is lost.*"

Words by LIZZIE EDWARDS. Music by JNO. R. SWENEY.

1. O hear the gos - pel mes - sage, With trumpet-tongue it rings;
2. He seeks for those who slight him, Be - canse of un - be - lief;
3. The way to him is sim - ple,—'Tis on - ly look and live;

What hope and con - so - la - tion To sin - ners lost it brings:
Who feel their sins a bur - den, But will not ask re - lief.
One step, and O how glad - ly His mer - cy will for - give.

No more like sheep we wan - der, With - out a shepherd's care,
In paths of gloom and dark - ness, Where wea - ry foot-steps roam,
'Twas not to call the right - eous, Our dear Re-deem-er came,

There is a fold, a precious fold, Whose ref - uge all may share.
He reach - es forth his lov-ing arms To bear the wand'rer home.
But hun - gry, starving, helpless ones: O praise his ho - ly name!

CHORUS.

The Son of Man has come, the lost to seek and save; We
has come

To Seek and Save. Concluded.

glory in his Cross, who triumph'd o'er the grave : O write it on his standard, That

o'er the earth shall wave, Behold the Son of Man has come The lost to seek and save!

232   Sing Again.

Words by LIZZIE EDWARDS.   Music by JNO. R. SWENEY.

1. Sing a - gain, O heart of mine, What the Lord has done for thee;
2. Sing a - gain the words so dear, Words that faith de - lights to sing;
3. Sing a - gain, O sing a - gain Pard-'ning grace and mer - cy free;
4. Sing a - gain of rest and love, Per - fect rest from ev - 'ry care,

Fine.

Sing a - gain his love di - vine, More than all the world to me.
Now their mu - sic let me hear, "Sim - ply to the cross I cling."
Sing with this thy sweet re-frain, "Near - er, O my God, to thee."
In the Christian's home a - bove, In the fields of E - den fair!

D.S. "Je - sus, lov - er of my soul, Let me to thy bo - som fly."

CHORUS.   *D.S.*

Sing a - mid the waves that roll, Till I lift my voice and cry—

Copyright, 1885, by Jno. R. SWENEY.

233   Meet Me There.

Words by H. E. BLAIR.

Music by WM. J. KIRKPATRICK.

1. On the hap-py golden shore, Where the faithful part no more, When the
2. Here our fondest hopes are vain, Dear-est links are rent in twain; But in
3. Where the harps of angels ring, And the blest for-ev-er sing, In the

storms of life are o'er, Meet me there. Where the night dissolves away In-to
heav'n no throb of pain, Meet me there. By the river sparkling bright, In the
pal-ace of the King, Meet me there. Where in sweet communion blend Heart
[with

D.S. storms of life are o'er, On the

pure and per-fect day, I am go-ing home to stay, Meet me there.
cit-y of delight, Where our faith is lost in sight, Meet me there.
heart, and friend with friend, In a world that ne'er shall end, Meet me there.

meet me there.

happy golden shore, Where the faithful part no more, Meet me there.

CHORUS.

Meet me there,   Meet me there,   Where the

Meet me there,   Meet me there,

Tree of Life is blooming, Meet me there. When the

Meet me there.

234 What shall I Sing for Thee?

Words by Rev. H. BURTON.

Music by JOSHUA GILL.

1. What shall I sing for thee, for thee, My Lord and Light? What shall I
2. Thou hast giv'n all for me, for me, Sav-iour Di - vine! I would give
3. Didst thou not die for me, for me, Ran-som for sin? Ascending on
4. What shall I do for thee, for thee, Glo - ri - ous Friend? Let me be
5. Then a still sweeter song, sweet song, Je - sus, I'll bring; Up 'mid the

bring to thee, to thee, Master, to - night? O for the strong de-sire!
all to thee, to thee, Ev - er-more thine! Let my heart cling to thee,
high for me, for me, Pleading with-in? All shall be dross for thee,
true to thee, to thee, Right to the end! Close to thy bleeding side,
ransom'd throng, blest throng, Then will I sing! Never to leave thee now,

O for the touch of fire! Then shall my tuneful lyre Praise thee a - right!
Let my lips sing for thee, Let me just bring to thee All that is mine!
All shall be loss for thee, Welcome the cross for thee, I, too, shall win!
Wash'd in the crimson tide, On till the waves divide, Till I as - cend!
Never to grieve thee now, Low at thy feet to bow, Won-der-ful King!

235 The Numberless Host.

F. A. B.

F. A. BLACKMER.

1. When we enter the portals of glo - ry, And the great host of ransom'd we see,
2. When we see all the sav'd of the a - ges, Who from cruel death partings are free,
3. When we stand by the beautiful riv - er, 'Neath the shade of the life-giving tree,
4. When we look on the form that redeem'd us, And his glory and majesty see,

As the numberless sand of the sea-shore, What a wonderful sight that will be!
Greeting there with a heavenly greeting, What a wonderful sight that will be!
Gazing out o'er the fair land of promise, What a wonderful sight that will be!
While as King of the saints he is reigning, What a wonderful sight that will be!

CHORUS.

Numberless as the sand of the sea - - - - shore, Num-ber-less

Numberless as the sand,

as the sand of the shore; Oh, what a sight 'twill be,

as the sand of the shore;

The Numberless Host. Concluded.

When the ransom'd host we see, As numberless as the sand of the sea-shore.

---

236   Now Bless Me.

Genesis 32: 26.

Wм. J. KIRKPATRICK.

1. I bring to thee, my Sav-iour, My weak and wand'ring heart; I can-not
2. I need thy cheering presence To guide me on my way; I need thy
3. I need thy cleansing Spir-it To wash me in thy blood, And fill me
4. I need thy Sa-cred likeness Up-on my heart impress'd; I need thy
5. I'm wea-ry with my bur-dens, I give my strivings o'er; I trust thy

CHORUS.

journey forward Till thou new strength impart. Now bless me, O bless me, I
full sal-va-tion To keep me day by day.
with thy nature, The per-fect will of God.
love re-kindled And burning in my breast.
blood to cleanse me, And save me ev-er-more.

will not let thee go; My soul shall grasp the promise, Till thou the gift bestow.

237 Beautiful Land.

W. J. K.

WM. J. KIRKPATRICK.

1. There's a land, beautiful land, just beyond, In the re-gion of boundless de-
2. In that land, beautiful land, just beyond, There will be neither sor-row nor
3. In that land, beautiful land, just beyond, There's a city whose streets are of
4. In that land, beautiful land, just beyond, Our Redeemer, the Lamb, we shall
5. To that land, beautiful land, we shall go, If our garments are spotless and

light, Where no darkness, nor cloud breaks the noontide of bliss: Where the sun ever
strife; We shall rest on the banks of the pure crystal stream, And partake of its
gold: Jasper walls, pearly gates, trees of life, mansions fair. We shall soon in their
see; King of kings, Lord of lords, over all He shall reign, And His brightness our
white; Leaving sorrow and sighing and toil-ing below, We shall soar to that

CHORUS.

shines clear and bright. Beautiful land, o-ver the strand, Beautiful
Wa - ter of Life.
gran - deur be-hold.
glo - ry shall be.
world of de-light.

Beautiful land, over the strand,

home of the faith-ful on high; Happy and blest, ev-er to

Happy and blest,

Beautiful Land. Concluded.

rest, ev-er to rest, We shall be there, o-ver there, by and by.

238 ## Remember Me.

Music and Chorus by Asa Hull.

1. A-las! and did my Sav-iour bleed? And did my Sov'reign die?
Cho.—Help me, dear Sav-iour, thee to own, And ev - er faith-ful be;

Would he de-vote that sa-cred head For such a worm as I?
And when thou sit-test on thy throne, Dear Lord, re-mem-ber me.

2 Was it for crimes that I have done,
He groaned upon the tree?
Amazing pity! grace unknown!
And love beyond degree!

3 Well might the sun in darkness hide,
And shut his glories in,
When Christ, the mighty Maker, died
For man, the creature's sin.

4 Thus might I hide my blushing face,
While his dear cross appears;
Dissolve my heart in thankfulness,
And melt mine eyes to tears.

5 But drops of grief can ne'er repay
The debt of love I owe;
Here, Lord, I give myself away,—
'Tis all that I can do.

239 WHENCE CAME THE ARMIES OF THE SKY?

1 Whence came the armies of the sky,
John saw in visions bright?
Whence came their crowns, their robes,
their palms,
Too pure for mortal sight?
Chorus.
They looked like men in uniform,
They looked like men of war;
They all were clad in armor bright,
And conqu'ring palms they bore.

2 Were these tried soldiers of the cross
Victorious in the fight?
Were these the trophies they had won,
Reserved in worlds of light?

3 Once they were mourners here below,
And poured out cries and tears;
They wrestled hard, as we do now,
With sins and doubts and fears.

4 They saw the Star of Bethlehem
Arise in splendor bright!
They followed long its guiding ray,
Till beamed a clearer light.

5 From desert waste and cities full,
From dungeons dark they've come,
And now they claim their mansion fair:
They've found their long-sought home.
Asa Hull, by per.

240   I am a poor Sinner, I know.

Words and Melody by GRACIE E. LOVELIGHT.

1. I am a poor sin-ner, I know;   I am a poor sin-ner, I
2. I am a poor sin-ner, I know;   But Je-sus had mer-cy on
3. I am a poor sin-ner, I know;   On Je-sus my burdens I
4. I am a poor sin-ner, I know;   But Je-sus from sin sets me
5. I am a poor sin-ner, I know;   But Christ is my joy and my

I know;

know; But Je-sus is mine, O rap-ture di-vine, His blood makes me
me; He pass'd me not by, but heard my sad cry, And now his sal-
roll; In him I be-lieve, from him I re-ceive Sweet comfort and
free; And while he is near, O why should I fear, His grace is suf-
song; I rest on his Word, my Saviour and Lord, Who ten-der-ly

whit-er than snow,   His blood makes me whit-er than snow.
va-tion I see,   And now his sal-va-tion I see.
peace to my soul,   Sweet com-fort and peace to my soul.
fi-cient for me,   His grace is suf-fi-cient for me.
leads me a-long,   Who ten-der-ly leads me a-long.

than snow.

241   Gloria Patri.

Glory be to the Father, and | to the | Son, ‖ and | to the | Holy | Ghost. ‖
As it was in the beginning, is now, and | ever | shall be, ‖ world | without |
end, A-| men.

242 His Grace is Abundant and Free.

Words by JOSHUA GILL.—Written for this Work.   Music by JNO. R. SWENEY.

1. Jesus saves me and keeps me from sin, By the blood that he shed on the
2. It is bless-ed his presence to feel, And his faithful dis-ci - ple to
3. In his care I am hap-py and blest, And his perfect peace flows unto
4. When in glo-ry the Saviour we meet, When the King in his beau-ty we

tree; Through his Spirit and Word I am clean, For his grace is a-
be; For his love he delights to re - veal, And his grace is a-
me, And my Spirit is always at rest, For his grace is a-
see, We'll con-fess as we fall at his feet That his grace is a-

CHORUS.

bundant and free. Yes, I know, Grace is free, For it

Yes, I know, Grace is free

cleanses and saves even me. Yes, I know,

E - ven me. Yes, I know, Grace is free,

Grace is free, For it cleanses and saves even me.

Yes, I know, Grace is free,

243   We Walk by Faith.

Words by FANNY J. CROSBY.   Music by WM. J. KIRKPATRICK.

We walk by faith, etc.

1. We walk by faith,......... and O how sweet........The flow'rs that
2. We walk by faith,......... he wills it so,.......... And marks the
3. We walk by faith,......... di-vine-ly blest,........ On him we
4. And thus by faith,......... till life shall end,........ We'll walk with

grow...... beneath our feet,......And fragrance breathe... along the
path......that we should go ;......And when, at times...... our sky is
lean,...... in him we rest ;......The more we trust.... our Shepherd's
him,...... our dearest Friend,.... Till safe we tread...... the fields of

way........ That leads the soul......... to end-less day.......
dim,........ He gently draws........ us close to him......
care,........ The more his love........ 'tis ours to share.....
light,....... Where faith is lost........ in per-fect sight.....

CHORUS.   express.

We walk by faith, but not a-lone, Our Shepherd's ten-der voice we hear,

We Walk by Faith. Concluded.

And feel his hand with-in our own, And know that he is al-ways near.

244   **Yatman. 8 lines. 7s.**

CHAS. WESLEY.   WM. J. KIRKPATRICK.

1. Je - sus, lov - er of my soul, Let me to thy bo - som fly,

While the near-er wat-ers roll, While the tem-pest still is high;

D.S. Safe in - to the ha - ven guide, O re - ceive my soul at last.

Hide me, O my Saviour, hide, Till the storm of life is past;

2 Other refuge have I none,
  Hangs my helpless soul on thee;
Leave, O leave me not alone,
  Still support and comfort me:
All my trust on thee is stayed,
  All my help from thee I bring;
Cover my defenceless head
  With the shadow of thy wing.

3 Thou, O Christ, art all I want;
  More than all in thee I find;
Raise the fallen, cheer the faint,
  Heal the sick, and lead the blind.

Just and holy is thy name;
  I am all unrighteousness;
False and full of sin I am:
  Thou art full of truth and grace.

4 Plenteous grace with thee is found,
  Grace to cover all my sin;
Let the healing streams abound,
  Make and keep me pure within.
Thou of life the fountain art,
  Freely let me take of thee;
Spring thou up within my heart,
  Rise to all eternity.

245 Lean Sweetly on Jesus.

Words by FANNY J. CROSBY.

Music by JNO. R. SWENEY.

1. Lean sweetly on Jesus, O child of his care, Each heart-throb of an-guish he
2. Lean sweetly on Jesus, he knoweth thy fears, Lean sweetly on Je-sus, he
3. Lean sweetly on Jesus, O child of his grace, Nor think for one mo-ment he
4. Lean sweetly on Jesus, O child of his love, How ten-der-ly o'er thee he
5. Lean sweetly on Jesus, what-ev-er be-fall; Go hide in his mer-cy, and

wait-eth to share; Lean sweetly on Jesus, when earth-skies are dim, When
se - eth thy tears: No friend like thy Saviour so deep-ly can feel, And
hid - eth his face; That soul-cheering promise is firm as his throne,—He
bends from a-bove; How kindly and gently he whispers to thee.— I
trust him for all; Hold fast to thy anchor, tho' earth-skies are dim, With

CHORUS.

stars veil their lus-tre, O cling thou to him. O cling...... thou to
tho' he may wound thee, 'tis on - ly to heal.
will not de - sert thee, nor leave thee a - lone.
am thy Re-deem-er, then rest thou in me.
faith nev - er fail - ing, a - bide now in him.

Lean sweetly on Jesus, O

him,...... O cling...... thou to him,...... Lean sweetly on

cling thou to him, Lean sweetly on Jesus, O cling thou to him,

Lean Sweetly on Jesus. Concluded.

ad lib.

Jesus, Lean sweetly on Jesus, Lean sweetly on Jesus, O cling thou to him.

---

246   **America.   6s & 4s.**

Words by Rev. S. F. Smith.   Adapted by Henry Carey, obit. 1743.

1. My country, 'tis of thee, Sweet land of liberty, Of thee I sing; Land where my
2. My native country! thee, Land of the noble free, Thy name I love: I love thy

fathers died, Land of the pilgrim's pride; From ev'ry mountain side Let freedom ring.
rocks and rills, Thy woods and templed hills; My heart with rapture thrills Like that
[above.

3
Let music swell the breeze,
And ring from all the trees
  Sweet freedom's song!
Let mortal tongues awake;
Let all that breathe partake;
Let rocks their silence break—
  The sound prolong.

4
Our fathers' God! to thee,
Author of liberty,
  To thee we sing;
Long may our land be bright
With freedom's holy light;
Protect us by thy might,
  Great God, our King!

---

247   MY FAITH LOOKS UP TO THEE.

1
My faith looks up to thee,
Thou Lamb of Calvary,
  Saviour divine,
Now hear me while I pray:
Take all my guilt away;
O let me from this day
  Be wholly thine.

2
May thy rich grace impart
Strength to my fainting heart;
  My zeal inspire;

As thou hast died for me,
O may my love to thee—
Pure, warm and changeless be,
  A living fire.

3
While life's dark maze I tread,
And griefs around me spread,
  Be thou my guide;
Bid darkness turn to day;
Wipe sorrow's tears away,
Nor let me ever stray
  From thee aside.   Ray Palmer.

248 Thinking of Home.

Words by LIZZIE EDWARDS. Music by JNO. R. SWENEY.

1. I am thinking of home in Im-man-u-el's land, A home that is
2. I am thinking of home and the Riv-er of Life That flows from the
3. I am thinking of home, where the gates are of pearl, No darkness e'er
4. I am thinking of home, and I look for the hour When he, my Re-

fade - less and fair, Where the pure and the blest from their labors shall rest : I
midst of the Throne : They shall hunger no more, neither thirst on that shore, Where
man - tles the skies ; And a Saviour's dear hand, in that beautiful land, Shall
deemer, shall come ! When the morning shall break, and my soul shall awake To

CHORUS.

know that my lov'd ones are there.   O - ver the sea, far o - ver the sea,
Je - sus will gath-er his own.
wipe ev-'ry tear from our eyes.
meet all the lov'd ones at home.

Voices are ten-der-ly call-ing to me: Call - ing to me,
Calling to me,   Calling to me,

Thinking of Home. Concluded.

call - - - ing to me,   O - - ver the jas - per sea.

Call-ing to me,   call-ing to me,   Over, yes, o - ver the jas - per sea.

249   I bring my Sins to Thee.

Words by Miss F. R. HAVERGAL.   Music by WM. J. KIRKPATRICK.

1. I bring my sins to thee, The sins I can-not count, That all may cleansed
2. I bring my grief to thee, The grief I can-not tell; No words shall needed
3. My joys to thee I bring, The joys thy love has given, That each may be a
4. My life I bring to thee, I would not be my own; O Saviour, let me

CHORUS.

be   In thy once opened Fount.   I bring them, Saviour, all to thee, The
be,   Thou knowest all so well: I bring the sor-row laid on me, O
wing   To lift me nearer heaven: I bring them, Saviour, all to thee, Who
be   Thine ev - er, thine a - lone: My heart, my life, my all   I bring To

bur-den is too great for me, The bur - den is too great for me.
suffering Saviour, all to thee, O suff - 'ring Saviour, all to thee.
hast procur'd them all for me, Who hast procur'd them all for me.
thee, my Saviour and my King, To thee, my Saviour and my King.

1. The burden is too great for me, too great, too great for me.
2. O suffering Saviour, all to thee, O Saviour, all to thee.
3. Who hast procur'd them all for me, Procur'd them all for me.
4. To thee, my Saviour and my King, My Saviour and my King.

Why Delay?

Words by LIZZIE EDWARDS.

Music by JNO. R. SWENEY.

1. To the fountain flow-ing free, Come a - way, come a - way; O there's
2. He has call'd thee o'er and o'er, Come a - way, come a - way; But he
3. Hast thou faith in Christ, the Lord, Come a - way, come a - way; Wilt thou

mer - cy there for thee, Why de - lay? why de - lay? From the
soon may call no more, Why de - lay? why de - lay? Tho' thy
take him at his word, Why de - lay? why de - lay? If re -

Sav-iour's bleed-ing side, At the cross, where once he died, See the
sins like bil - lows roll, Tho' their weight oppress thy soul, If thou
pent - ing, thou be - lieve, And no more the Spir - it grieve, Then his

D.S. fountain, flow - ing free, To the blood that cleanseth me, Where the

Fine. CHORUS.

bless-ed heal-ing tide, Flowing free, flowing free. Come, sinner, come, the
wilt, he'll make thee whole. Come a - way, come a - way.
love thou shalt re-ceive. Come a - way, come a - way.

Saviour waits for thee, Come a - way, come a - way.

Why Delay? Concluded.

rit.   D.S.

m,ments fly a - pace, Soon, ah, too soon may end thy day of grace ; To the

---

251   Turner. C. M.   MAXIM.

1. Awake, my soul! stretch ev'ry nerve, And press with vig - or on:

A heav'nly race de-mands thy zeal, A heav'nly race de -
A heav'nly race de-mands thy zeal, And

heav'nly race de - mands thy zeal, And an im - mor-tal

mands thy zeal, And an im-mor-tal crown. A heav'nly race demands thy zeal,
an im - mor - - - tal crown.

crown, And an im - mor-tal crown.

And an im - mor-tal crown.

2 'Tis God's all-animating voice
    That calls thee from on high;
 'Tis he whose hand presents the prize
    To thine aspiring eye.
3 A cloud of witnesses around
    Hold thee in full survey;
 Forget the steps already trod,
    And onward urge thy way.
4 Blest Saviour! introduced by thee,
    Our race have we begun;
 And, crown'd with vict'ry, at thy feet
    We'll lay our trophies down.

252 I Believe Jesus Saves.

Words by Rev. W. McDonald.　　　　　　　　　　Music by J. P. Webster.

1. I am com-ing to Je-sus for rest, Rest, such as the
2. In com-ing, my sin I de-plore, My weak-ness and
3. To Je-sus I give up my all, Ev-'ry treasure and
4. I am trust-ing in Je-sus a-lone, Trust-ing now his sal-
5. My heart is in rap-tures of love, Love, such as the

pu-ri-fied know; My soul is a-thirst to be blest, To be
pov-er-ty show; I long to be sav'd ev-er-more, To be
i-dol I know; For his ful-ness of bless-ing I call, Till his
va-tion to know; And his blood doth so ful-ly a-tone, I am
ransom'd ones know; I am strengthen'd with might from a-bove, I am

CHORUS.

wash'd and made whit-er than snow. I be-lieve Je-sus
wash'd and made whit-er than snow.
blood wash-es whit-er than snow.
wash'd and made whit-er than snow.
wash'd and made whit-er than snow.

I be-lieve Je-sus

saves, And his blood washes whit-er than snow. I be-
saves, Je-sus saves, Je-sus saves, I be-

Melody used by permission of Oliver Ditson & Co.　　　*Words written for this Work.*

lieve   Je-sus saves,   And his blood washes whiter than snow.

lieve Je-sus saves, I be-lieve Je-sus saves,

---

253 **I HAVE ENTERED THE VALLEY OF BLESSING SO SWEET.**
(No. 73 in " BEULAH SONGS.")

1 I have entered the valley of blessing so sweet,
And Jesus abides with me there;
And his spirit and blood make my cleansing complete,
And his perfect love casteth out fear.

Chorus.

Oh come to this valley of blessing so sweet,
Where Jesus will fulness bestow—
And believe, and receive, and confess him,
That all his salvation may know.

2 There is peace in the valley of blessing so sweet,
And plenty the land doth impart;
And there's rest for the weary worn traveler's feet,
And joy for the sorrowing heart.

3 There is love in the valley of blessing so sweet, [may feel,
Such as none but the blood-wash'd
When heaven comes down redeemed spirits to greet,
And Christ sets his covenant seal.

4 There's a song in the valley of blessing so sweet
That angels would fain join the strain,
As with rapturous praises we bow at his feet, [slain !"
Crying, "Worthy the Lamb that was

---

254 **DEAR JESUS, I LONG TO BE PERFECTLY WHOLE.**
(No. 26 in " BEULAH SONGS.")

1 Dear Jesus, I long to be perfectly whole;
I want thee forever to live in my soul:
Break down every idol, cast out every foe;
Now wash me, and I shall be whiter than snow.

Chorus.

Whiter than snow, yes, whiter than snow:
Now wash me, and I shall be whiter than snow.

2 Dear Jesus, let nothing unholy remain;
Apply thine own blood, and remove every stain:
To have this blest cleansing, I all things forego:
Now wash me, and I shall be whiter than snow.

3 Dear Jesus, come down from thy throne in the skies,
And help me to make a complete sacrifice;
I give up myself, and whatever I know:
Now wash me, and I shall be whiter than snow.

4 Dear Jesus, thou seest I patiently wait;
Come now and within me a clean heart create:
To those who have sought thee thou never saidst no,
Now wash me, and I shall be whiter than snow.

5 Dear Jesus, for this I most humbly entreat;
I wait, blessed Lord, at thy crucified feet;
By faith, for my cleansing, I see thy blood flow:
Now wash me, and I shall be whiter than snow.

6 The blessing, by faith, I receive from above:
O glory! my soul is made perfect in love:
My prayer has prevailed, and this moment I know
The blood is applied: I am whiter than snow.   J. NICHOLSON,

255   Room for the World.

Words by CHARLES H. ELLIOT.   Music by JNO. R. SWENEY.

1. Room for the world at the cross of the Saviour, Room where forgiveness he
2. Room for the world in the fold of the Saviour, Room at the feast by his
3. Room for the world in the ark of the Saviour, Yon-der the tempest is
4. Room for the world in the arms of the Saviour, Room for the friendless, the

waits to bestow; Room where so many have laid down their burdens, Room at the
mer - cy prepar'd; Come ye that hunger, his bounty receiving, Feed on the
sweep - ing a-pace; No one but Jesus can shield and defend you, Haste to the
lone and oppress'd; There will he comfort the poor and forsaken, There to the

CHORUS.

waters of cleansing that flow. Say, will you come, the Spirit now is pleading;
blessings that millions have shar'd.
shel - ter and ref - uge of Grace.
wea - ry he giveth sweet rest.

Je - sus a-bove for you is in-ter-ceding: Why will you still, his

Room for the World. *Concluded.*

tender love unheeding, Per - ish for - ev - er in sight of the cross?

---

256   Wand'rer, Welcome Home.

Words by WM. H. CLARK.   Music by WM. J. KIRKPATRICK.

1. To thy Father's house returning, Wand'rer, haste away; Lo, his heart for
2. In thy Father's house is wait-ing Plenty and to spare; Why with hunger
3. Why in for-eign lands a stranger, Wilt thou longer roam? Rise at once, thy
4. Lo, he waits and longs to greet thee, Longs thy soul to bless; Come, repenting,
5. He will soothe thy ev - 'ry sorrow, Calm thy ev'-ry fear; Robe thee in the

thee is yearning, Why so long de - lay?
wilt thou per-ish, Now his boun-ty share.
Father calls thee, "Haste, my child, come home."
seek his par-don, Now thy sin con - fess.
precious garment Of his love so dear.

REFRAIN.

Wand-'rer, wand-'rer,

Quickly, quickly come; Wand'rer, wand'rer, Welcome, welcome home!

Sitting at the Feet of Jesus.

Words by J. H.

Music arranged for this Work.

1. Sit - ting at the feet of Je-sus, O what words I hear him say!
2. Sit - ting at the feet of Je-sus, Where can mor-tal be more blest?
3. Bless me, O my Saviour, bless me, As I sit low at thy feet;

Hap - py place! so near, so precious! May it find me there each day:
There I lay my sins and sorrows, And, when wea-ry, find sweet rest:
Oh look down in love up - on me, Let me see thy face so sweet,

Sit - ting at the feet of Je - sus, I would look up - on the past;
Sit - ting at the feet of Je - sus, There I love to weep and pray,
Give me, Lord, the mind of Je - sus, Make me ho - ly as he is;

For his love has been so gra-cious, It has won my heart at last.
While I from his fulness gath-er Grace and comfort ev - 'ry day.
May I prove I've been with Je-sus, Who is all my righteousness.

---

258   COME, YE SINNERS POOR AND NEEDY.

1 Come, ye sinners, poor and needy,
  Weak and wounded, sick and sore;
Jesus ready stands to save you,
  Full of pity, love and power.
  ‖: He is able, he is able,
  He is willing: doubt no more. :‖

2 Now, ye needy, come and welcome;
  God's free bounty glorify;
True belief and true repentance—
  Every grace that brings you nigh—
  ‖: Without money, without money,
  Come to Jesus Christ and buy. :‖

3 Let not conscience make you linger,
  Nor of fitness fondly dream;
All the fitness he requireth
  Is to feel your need of him.
  ‖: This he gives you, this he gives you,
  'Tis the Spirit's glimm'ring beam. :‖

4 Come, ye weary, heavy laden,
  Bruised and mangled by the fall,
If you tarry till you're better,
  You will never come at all.
  ‖: Not the righteous, not the righteous,
  Sinners, Jesus came to call. :‖

I always go to Jesus.

ANON.   J. S. HARTT.

1. I always go to Jesus: When troubled or distress'd, I always find a
2. When full of dread forboding, And flowing o'er with tears, He calms away my
3. When those are cold and faithless Who once were fond and true, With careless
[hearts for-

ref-uge Up-on his lov-ing breast; I tell him all my tri-als, I
sor-row And hushes all my fears; He comprehends my weakness, The
sa-king The old friends for the new. I turn to him whose friendship Knows

tell him all my grief; And, while my lips are speaking, He gives my heart relief.
per-il I am in, And he supplies the ar-mor I need to conquer sin.
neither change nor end: I always find in Je-sus A never-failing friend.

CHORUS.

I al-ways go to Jesus: When troubled or distress'd, I al-ways find a

4

refuge Up-on his loving breast.

I always go to Jesus:
No matter when or where
I seek his gracious presence,
I'm sure to find him there.
In times of joy or sorrow,
Whate'er my need may be,
I always go to Jesus,
And Jesus comes to me.

Will You Come?

Words by CARRIE M. WILSON. Music by JNO. R. SWENEY.

1. There's a message from the Lord, Will you come? Hear it sounding from his
2. He has tarried long for you, Will you come? See, his locks are wet with
3. Will you heed the Saviour's call? Will you come? To the feast prepar'd for

Word, Will you come? Whoso-ev - er on his name will be-lieve, Life e -
dew, Will you come? He a-lone your many sins can for-give, Will you
all, Will you come? You will find him at the cross, waiting there, With the

CHORUS.

ter-nal shall from him receive. He is calling you to-day, will you come?
look to him by faith and live?
garment that your soul must wear.

will you come

To the on-ly living way, will you come? Will you plunge beneath the

will you come

Will You Come? Concluded.

flood Of his all - atoning blood? Will you be a child of God? Will you come?

---

261 **Russia. L. M.**

READ.

1. Lord, how secure and blest are they Who feel the joys of par-don'd sin;

Should storms of wrath shake earth and sea, Their

Should storms of wrath shake Their

Should storms of wrath shake earth and sea, Their minds have heav'n and

minds have heav'n and peace with-in.

earth and sea, Their minds have heav'n and peace within.

minds have heav'n and peace with-in.

peace with - in.

2 The day glides sweetly o'er their heads,
Made up of innocence and love;
And, soft and silent as the shades,
Their nightly minutes gently move.

3 Quick as their thoughts, their joys come on
But fly not half so swift away;
Their souls are ever bright as noon,
And calm as summer evenings be.

4 How oft they look to the heavenly hills,
Where groves of living pleasure grow;
And longing hopes, and cheerful smiles,
Sit undisturb'd upon their brow.

5 They scorn to seek earth's golden toys,
But spend the day, and share the night
In numb'ring o'er the richer joys
That heaven prepares for their delight.

213

262   Jesus, Mighty to Save!

Words by MAMIE PAYNE.   Music by JNO. R. SWENEY.

1. I wander'd a-far from God and from home, Oft wreck'd by the billows, and
2. He saw my despair, for danger was near, My sails were all shatter'd, I
3. My child, it is I, in pit-y he said, Then be of good comfort, O
4. And now in his love while sweetly I dwell, The news of sal-va-tion to

toss'd by the foam ; A prey to the storm-king by night and by day, No
trem-bled with fear ; My ves-sel was sinking, when lo! on the wave, He
lift up thy head; The old ship of Zi-on is wait-ing for thee, Make
oth-ers I tell: For he, my Pre-serv-er, when wreck'd on the wave, Is

rud-der, no compass, fast drift-ing a-way.
came to my res-cue, the Mighty to Save!
haste while she lingers, and trust thou in me.
read-y and willing, and Mighty to Save!

CHORUS.

He is mighty to

save,   Yes, he is mighty to save,

Mighty to save,   Mighty to save,

Jesus, Mighty to Save. Concluded.

O, glo-ry to God, glo-ry to God, Christ is Mighty to Save!

---

263 **Penitence.** **7s, 6s & 8s.** W. H. OAKLEY.

1. Vain, de-lu-sive world, a - dieu, With all of crea-ture good;

On-ly Je-sus I pur-sue, Who bought me with his blood.

D.S. On-ly Je-sus will I know, And Je-sus cru-ci-fied!

Fine.

D.S.

All thy pleasures I fore-go, I trample on thy wealth and pride;

2 Other knowledge I disdain:
   'Tis all but vanity:
Christ, the Lamb of God, was slain,—
   He tasted death for me.
Me to save from endless woe,
   The sin-atoning Victim died:
Only Jesus will I know,
   And Jesus crucified.

3 Here will I set up my rest;
   My fluctuating heart
From the haven of his breast
   Shall never more depart:
Whither should a sinner go?
   His wounds for me stand open wide;
Only Jesus will I know,
   And Jesus crucified.

4 Him to know is life and peace,
   And pleasure without end;
This is all my happiness,
   On Jesus to depend:
Daily in his grace to grow,
   And ever in his faith abide:
Only Jesus will I know,
   And Jesus crucified.

5 O that I could all invite,
   This saving truth to prove;
Show the length, the breadth, the height
   And depth of Jesus' love!
Fain I would to sinners show
   The blood by faith alone applied:
Only Jesus will I know,
   And Jesus crucified.

264 Along the River of Time.

"Remember how short time is."—Ps. 89: 47.

GEO. F. ROOT.   GEO. F. ROOT.

1. A - long the Riv - er of Time we glide, A - long the Riv - er, a -
2. A - long the Riv - er of Time we glide, A - long the Riv - er, a -
3. A - long the Riv - er of Time we glide, A - long the Riv - er, a -

long the Riv-er, The swift-ly flow-ing, re - sist - less tide, The
long the Riv-er; A thou-sand dan-gers its cur-rents hide, A
long the Riv-er; Our Sav-iour on - ly our bark can guide, Our

swift - ly flowing, the swift - ly flow-ing, And soon, ah, soon, the
thou-sand dangers, a thou-sand dangers, And near our course the
Sav - iour on - ly, our Sav-iour on - ly, But with him we se -

end we'll see: Yes, soon 'twill come, and we will be
rocks we see: Oh, dread - ful thought! a wreck to be,
cure may be: No fear, no doubt, but joy to be

Floating, Floating Out on the sea of e - ter - ni - ty!

If a single voice sings this, let it change from the Tenor lines to the Soprano.

Along the River of Time.

pp   *rit.*

Floating, Floating Out on the sea of E - ter - ni-ty!

---

265   All of Thee.

Words by Rev. THEO. MONOD.   Music by WM. J. KIRKPATRICK,

1. O the bit-ter shame and sorrow, That a time could ev - er be,
2. Yet he found me, I be-held him Bleed-ing on th' ac-cur - sed tree:
3. Day by day his ten-der mer-cy, Heal-ing, help-ing, full and free,
4. High-er than the highest heaven, Deep - er than the deep-est sea,

When I let the Saviour's pit - y Plead in vain, and proudly answer'd
Heard him pray, forgive them, Father, And my wistful heart said, faintly,
Sweet and strong, and oh so patient, Brought me lower, while I whisper'd
Lord, thy love at last has conquer'd : Grant me now my soul's de-sire,

All of self, and none of thee. All of self, and none of thee.
Some of self, and some of thee. Some of self, and some of thee.
Less of self, and more of thee. Less of self, and more of thee.
None of self, and all of thee. None of self, and all of thee.

266   Jesus is Passing this Way.

Words by E. A. H.

Music by J. H. TENNEY. By per.

1. Is there a sin-ner a - wait-ing Mer-cy and pardon to - day?
2. Brother, the Master is wait - ing, Waiting to free-ly for - give;
3. Yes, he is coming to bless you, While in contrition you bow;

Welcome the news that we bring him: "Jesus is passing this way!"
Why not this moment ac - cept him, Trust in his grace and live?
Com-ing from sin to re - deem you, Read-y to save you now;

Coming in love and in mer - cy, Pardon and peace to be - stow,
He is so tender and pre - cious, He is so near you to - day;
Can you refuse the sal - va - tion Je-sus is of - fer-ing here?

Coming to save the poor sin - ner From his heart-anguish and woe.
Open your heart to re - ceive him, While he is passing this way.
Open your heart to ad - mit him, While he is coming so near.

CHORUS.

Je-sus is passing this way, ... To - day, ... to - day, ...

Jesus is passing this way, To-day, is passing to-day!

While he is near, O be - lieve him, Open your heart to re - ceive him, For

Je-sus is passing this way,.... Is passing this way to - day.
this way,

---

267 JESUS, MY LORD, TO THEE I CRY.
(No. 28 in "Beulah Songs.")

1 Jesus, my Lord, to thee I cry,
Unless thou help me, I must die;
Oh, bring thy free salvation nigh,
And take me as I am!

Cho.—Take me as I am,
Take me as I am!
Oh, bring thy free salvation nigh,
And take me as I am!

2 Helpless I am, and full of guilt,
But yet for me thy blood was spilt,
And thou can'st make me what thou wilt,
But take me as I am! [wilt,

3 No preparation can I make,
My best resolves I only break,

Yet save me for thine own name's sake,
And take me as I am!

4 I thirst, I long to know thy love,
Thy full salvation I would prove;
But since to thee I cannot move,
Oh, take me as I am!

5 If thou hast work for me to do,
Inspire my will, my heart renew,
And work both in and by me too,
But take me as I am!

6 And when at last the work is done,
The battle o'er, the vict'ry won,
Still, still my cry shall be alone,—
Lord, take me as I am!

---

268 Hamburg. L. M.

1. Just as I am, with-out one plea, But that thy blood was shed for me,

And that thou bid'st me come to thee, O Lamb of God, I come, I come!

2 Just as I am, and waiting not
To rid my soul of one dark blot; [spot,
To thee, whose blood can cleanse each
O Lamb of God, I come!

3 Just as I am, though tossed about
With many a conflict, many a doubt;
Fightings within, and fears without,
O Lamb of God, I come!

4 Just as I am, poor, wretched, blind,
Sight, riches, healing of the mind,

Yea, all I need in thee to find,
O Lamb of God, I come!

5 Just as I am, thou wilt receive,
Wilt welcome, pardon, cleanse, relieve,
Because thy promise I believe,
O Lamb of God I come!

6 Just as I am, thy love unknown
Hath broken every barrier down;
Now to be thine, and thine alone,
O Lamb of God, I come!

Adoration.

Words by H. M. BRADLY. Arranged by Rev. W. McDONALD.

1. Down in the val-ley, a - mong the sweet grasses, Walks my Be-
2. Know'st thou I seek thee? O haste to dis - cov-er The place of thy
3. Now I approach thee, O fair - est Re-deem-er! Lur'd by thy
4. Gen - tler thy voice than the whis-per of an-gels,— Bright-er thy

lov - ed,— his foot-prints I see; Haste I to fol - low him,
shel - ter'd and fra - grant re-treat, Where thou dost rest with thy
beau - ty to dwell in thy love: Hide not thy face from the
smile than the sun in the sky; Gath - er me ten - der - ly,

Sav - iour and Lover, How the winds whisper thy dear name to me.
flocks at the noontide, By fountains of water, unsearch'd by the heat.
heart that adores thee; Have I not sought thee, and found thee, my "Dove?"
close to thy bosom, Faint with thy love-li-ness—there let me die.

270 ## Zion. 8s, 7s & 4s. THOMAS HASTINGS.

Welcome, welcome, dear Redeemer! Welcome to this heart of mine! }
Lord, I make a full sur-ren-der, Ev'ry pow'r and tho't be thine: } Thine en-

tirely;—thro' e-ter-nal ages thine. Thine entirely; thro' e-ter-nal a-ges thine.

271 LORD, DISMISS US WITH THY BLESSING.

1 Lord, dismiss us with thy blessing,
Fill our hearts with joy and peace;
Let us each, thy love possessing,
Triumph in redeeming grace:
O refresh us,
Traveling through this wilderness.
2 Thanks we give, and adoration,
For thy Gospel's joyful sound;
May the fruits of thy salvation

In our hearts and lives abound;
May thy presence
With us evermore be found.
3 So, whene'er the signal's given,
Us from earth to call away,
Borne on angels' wings to heaven,
Glad the summons to obey,
May we ever
Reign with Christ in endless day.

220 WALTER SHIRLEY.

INDEX.